Unearthing the Diamond

A Story of Struggle and Strife to a Successful Life

Tamika Felina Pommells Williams

Tamika Felina Pommells Williams

Disclaimer

The information contained in this book is for general information purposes only. The information is provided by Tamika Felina Pommells Williams and while we endeavour to keep the information up to date and correct, we make no representations or warranties of any kind, express or implied, about the completeness, accuracy, reliability, suitability or availability with respect to this publication or the information, products, services, or related graphics contained in this publication for any purpose. Any reliance you place on such information is therefore strictly at your own risk.

In no event will we be liable for any loss or damage including without limitation, indirect or consequential loss or damage, or any loss or damage whatsoever arising from loss of data or profits arising out of, or in connection with, the use of this publication. Through this publication you are able to link to other resources and contacts which are not under the control of Tamika Felina Pommells Williams. We have no control over the nature, content and availability of those responsible for their management, operation or function. The inclusion of any links does not necessarily imply a recommendation or endorse the views expressed within them. At the time of writing, every effort was made to keep the information in this publication current. However, Tamika Felina Pommells Williams takes no responsibility for, and will not be liable for, information being out of date or unavailable due to technical or any other issue beyond our control.

To contact Tamika:

Telephone: (+1 876) 578 2582/807 4347

Email: Tamika@rasnatango.com, tamikafelina@gmail.com

Copyright Year: April 2016

Copyright Notice: by Tamika Felina Pommells Williams/Baobab Tree Books. All rights reserved. No part of this book may be reproduced in any form, or, by any means whatsoever.

Results in this copyright notice:
© 2016 Baobab Tree Books. All rights reserved.

ISBN: 978-1-909389-07-6

Unearthing the Diamond

A Story of Struggle and Strife to a Successful Life

Tamika Felina Pommells Williams

Dedication

My son, Ayale. This book explains so much about me, the things I felt I could never tell you and the things I should've said when you became a man. I decided when you were born I would always be supportive of you and swore to never abandon you. I promised God I would raise you to be a good man for your future partner and teach you to appreciate the simpler things in life. And when the/that time is RIGHT, you WILL find the right woman for you. Thank you for being my son. I love you and hope you will cherish the experiences I am about to share with you. *"Experience is the mother of learning."* So they say! What they forgot to add was, "it doesn't always have to be your experience". I love you and appreciate you.

Always and forever,

Mom

Unearthing the Diamond

Contents

Acknowledgements	5
Introduction	7
The Beginning	11
Finding Dad	29
On The Move	69
Our Son, Ayale	86
The Big "C"	106
He's Awake	113
Survival	124
Montego Bay, Here We Come!	131
Hurricane Gilbert	145
Ahhh...Ras Natango Garden & Gallery	164
Empowerment	175
From Rocks to Paradise	202
Epilogue	213

Tamika Felina Pommells Williams

Acknowledgements

I started writing this book in 2009 and tried in so many ways to get it published but to no avail since it was an unusual story. So special acknowledgement to Baobab Tree Books and Kwame MA McPherson who decided to listen believe and publish this book. The rest is, as they say, history. I always thought there were three men in my life but now there is a fourth and I must acknowledge them all. Ian, for coming up with the title and for painting me the diamond for the book's back, for loving me through it all, you are definitely my better half; Ayale, my son, for teaching me what unconditional love is. I am so proud of your artistic skills and gentle spirit; Mark Tucci, for loving me and knowing my thoughts without me even opening my mouth. My gratitude and thanks goes to my three musketeers. My newest and fourth Musketeer, Kwame MA McPherson, who has taken me on a roller coaster ride of highs and lows, laughter and tears, and for stressing that HEALING is still taking place. To all victims, I acknowledge you. I know your pain. To everyone who

Unearthing the Diamond

is about to take this journey with me, I acknowledge you.

Tamika Felina Pommells Williams

Tamika Felina Pommells Williams

Introduction

I am Tamika Felina Pommells Williams. I was named Leyla Felina Pommells at birth but later on in my life changed it to Tamika, by deed poll.

"Nothing changes one's fortune like a change of name or a change of place", is one of my husband's favourite sayings.

I was born on the 25th October 1961 to Mavis Francis and Felix Pommells. My mother moved to England leaving our dad behind with five children.

I am sharing my experiences with the hope of touching/reaching anyone who may have gone or going through, similar experiences and learn from mine. I have taken off the mask so you can all see the real me, as I am, a woman, a mere mortal. After all, it is not the experiences that shape our lives or our future, but our reaction to these experiences.

I have chosen to see the good in every experience you will read here.

I am who I am because of all those experiences (and I mean ALL of my experiences) and try to make sure my little light shines brightly within them. Those little lights made stronger by my angels. Yes, I do believe in ANGELS! They are everywhere! Every step along the way they have been there for me; especially one in particular - my true, guardian angel, Ian - my partner, husband and BEST friend).

It has taken me over thirty years to open some of those doors I had locked so securely, in the hope of never needing to revisit the pain. But to truly enjoy the greatest of life's pleasures, I MUST unlock those doors. It is Spring 2009 and in my mind, body and soul I am doing my 'spring cleaning'.

Get to know me, love me, cry with me, laugh with me but don't pity me. I am STRONG! I have survived and I want everyone who reads this book to take a look at themselves and realize we are who we choose to be. For many years I played with the idea of writing my life story, often starting to write in many notebooks that I eventually threw down somewhere around my home. When Rochelle (my son's ex-wife) suddenly stormed into our lives, I was forced to look at myself.

Tamika Felina Pommells Williams

How else could I give advice if I was still hurting or even afraid to look at my own past?

I want you to come with me on my journey!

Rochelle. She married my son but she carried so much pain. I desperately felt I needed to help her and tried everything to get her to open up and talk about her past, but she remained tight-lipped. It was obvious that whatever her experiences had been, they were literally eating away at her. I got the feeling from her that she was unable to communicate with me and must have thought I would not understand since my life seemed to be stable and carefree.

In an effort to reach her, I began telling her about my own experiences. She would listen but still felt the world owed her a favour. So, to reach out to her, I decided to revisit my own experiences, with the view of helping her to heal.

I did this without knowing that my experiences were helping me to heal. Yes, I deliberately started this book to show Rochelle that she CAN triumph over any situation. I am also writing this book for me as I clean the clutter from my own mind.

Unearthing the Diamond

There is an anonymous quote forwarded on the internet about the people who come into your life: *"Some people come into your life for a reason, a season or a lifetime."*

I've learnt to accept the people who came into my life be it for a reason, a season or a lifetime. Realizing my total acceptance and recognizing the role each new person plays within it. To all the women in my life, to all the women and men who will read this book, it's time to stop the violence against ourselves and to each other. It's time to live!

Nothing in life is impossible and I am NO LONGER afraid! This is who I am. - ME!

Tamika Felina Pommells Williams

The Beginning

Growing up in the country with my grandparents holds many memories. They were very strict and we weren't allowed to go to our neighbours' homes alone. In the 1960's the "entire village raised the child" and children weren't allowed to play at each other's homes. The only time we were able to do so was when we went to church, school or visited as a family.

Every Saturday we had a ritual - cleaning the house. We had to move all the furniture around in order to give it the weekly clean; it would take five of us - Patrick, Cecile, Denny, Laurence and I - all day. Pat being the eldest was responsible for cleaning the huge rug in the living room. There was no vacuum cleaner, just a strong stick and a broom. Denny and Larry cleaned the veranda; Cecile took care of the kitchen. I washed the bathroom and we all had to clean the entire house. This entails, wiping the floors with a mop then applying polish with a piece of cloth by hand, afterwards shining the floor with coconut

Unearthing the Diamond

brushes (a dry coconut cut across the middle, leaving fine fibres that act as a brush).

The house was the biggest house in the village and most people said we were the richest family in the community.

My grandfather, Haughton Bona Francis was born on a Spanish plantation (a slave boy, his mother worked in the kitchen). He was tall, dark and a very handsome man. The little finger on his right hand could not bend and even when he made a fist or wrote his name, it stuck out to the side.

He could only identify and write his name; people today would say he was illiterate but he was the most intelligent man I ever knew. He was always quoting Bible verses and was able to recall the book, chapter and verse he wanted to quote. Mom often read to him too.

Grandpa Haughton, who we called 'Dad', worked very hard and acquired many large parcels of land and by the sweat of his brow, and the work of his own hands, built an empire for himself and his family, even owning shares in the Jamaica Coffee Industry Board. He was definitely a businessman.

One of his beliefs was that one should have friends from all walks of life and would often say: *"A friend to write a letter, a friend to help you financially, a friend to do physical work for you, a friend to listen"!* To me it sounded like I needed a friend for everything. He did lead by example though and had friends who were very influential, professional, rich as well as poor.

We were exposed to it all.

Our family was the envy of the community and those in the village believed it was through Black Magic, such as *obeah* (obeah is the art of black magic which was supposedly inherited from our African descendants who were slaves. Haiti is well known for voodoo while obeah is the Jamaican word for black magic that made him successful and not through hard work and an ambition to support his family.

He met and married my grandmother, Mary Ann Howell, at an early age and the union produced seven children. All of whom became professionals in their own right. Uncle Azie - a trucker, Uncle Wilbert - a teacher, Uncle Laurel - a lawyer and Jamaica's ambassador to Switzerland, Uncle Irvin - a politician, Aunt Edna - psychiatrist, Aunt Freddie - a teacher/vice principal and our mom, Mavis - a nurse.

Dad worked very hard to give all his children the formal education he lacked. He was determined they would succeed and he often said to us, his grandchildren: *"Learn all you can while you are young or you will regret it when you are a man."*

It seemed he always had a phrase or quote for every argument or situation. Frequently, when threatening to give me a beating he would say: *"If I beat you today your bottom will be as white as a Lilly in the garden."*

They were a happy couple and after raising their seven children, here they were raising five grandchildren. We were blessed to be raised by them even though 'Dad' was very hard whenever he disciplined us.

Tamika Felina Pommells Williams

Our home was on eleven acres of land. It was a farm with cows, goats, pigs, chickens and even a mule named Fire Boy. Dad owned other lands and all his properties had names: Cumberland was cultivated with coffee; Lambow with plantains, avocado and bananas; Tricey with sugar cane and ground provisions; Pecan with a little of everything - peas, pumpkin, bananas, etc.

Dad often showered us with gifts but they came with many responsibilities. He would give us a goat and whoever got this animal was now responsible for its complete upkeep and existence. I recall him giving me a yam head to plant in a yam bank he prepared. When the yam was ready to be reaped he made sure I did so and carried it home to Mom. When I started living with Ian this proved priceless because I was able to identify yams growing in the wild and when they matured enough to be eaten. Eventually, and later on in my life, I was even able to teach Ian how to dig them up!

The eleven acres on which we lived was planted with citrus: orange, tangerine, ortanique, grapefruit and coconut trees. We often used dry coconuts to make coconut drops, cooking oil and custard which we ate with cooked green bananas. The property was on a hill and at the bottom ran a river with a large swimming hole we affectionately called The Basin. Saturday evenings after cleaning we would all go down to basin and bathe.

Pat was the one who first began diving off a high rock and into the deep end. A quiet mischief maker, we all saw him as Dad's favourite. Pat would often get out of his chores by saying he had to study and that worked on dad every time.

Cecile looked exactly like our mother and was Mama's favourite. Sometimes I hated her. She would always get us into trouble with Mom and often told Dad about whatever mischief we were up to. That usually ended with me getting a beating. Her hair was very short while mine was long. She would pull my hair until it hurts. Her hair was so short it would take Mom a long time to comb it and it would always be in plaits. Mine was mostly in one, two or three plaits.

One day she brushed her hair back and put two tiny plaits at the back. I would never forget the crushed look on her face when Dad saw it.

"Go and comb your hair! You think you're a big woman?" Cecile cried and said it wasn't fair.

"Leyla's hair is always combed in one or two." I snickered and laughed making sure Dad didn't see me. I really wished we had a better relationship growing up but I didn't want her around me. She ALWAYS told on me and we couldn't get along most of the times.

Denny was so sad at times. I think he missed our Dad as much as I did and so he was very hard on himself. As his little sister, I was very bright in school and in our home that was a no-no for Dad. Denny was the one I loved the most. He was a year older than me. It was very difficult with him being older than me and I was "brighter". It was no fault of his. He had the hardest work of us all and this manifested itself in him wetting his bed way into his teenage years.

Unearthing the Diamond

Larry was the baby of the bunch and we used to call him "baby baggy baggy sugar dumpling".

Denny, Larry and I shared the same parents and though we all doted on Larry, even as a small girl, my heart was with Denny. I wished I could have helped him with all his chores, but I had mine in the house, while he had his in the fields. Pat could cook, clean and wash. Every Sunday we took pleasure in chasing a rooster for dinner. Denny or Pat would put the rooster under a basket, hold onto its head and using a sharp machete, lop off its head in one sweep. On a nearby wood fire, a boiling pot of water waited to stick the rooster in and so doing, make it easier to remove the feathers.

Once this was done, Cecile and I were taught to gut the rooster - which meant cutting an opening between its legs; sticking our hands in to remove the stomach and of course, making sure NOT to burst the bitter gall (this was a small sack filled with a bitter green liquid attached to the liver). Pat would be the one cooking dinner and if the rooster was tough (hard to cook) he would add a rusty nail to it and this always seemed to work. He was the best cook and with Mama cooking all week, this was Pat's way to lessen her load.

We all went to Sunday school. Dad and Mama would join us later for Sunday worship. We all attended The John's Hall Baptist Church.

Monday through Friday was school. We were NEVER absent or late but if we were sick, we would have to stay home. We had to move the goats and water the cows before breakfast and still had to be early for school.

In school, we were the only children who wore shoes while all the other children came to school barefooted. We would take off our shoes and socks, put them in our bags and spend the day also barefooted. In the evenings we would put them back onto our dirty feet and go home. Now that I am a grown woman, I realized Mama knew because our socks were always dirty but she never said a word.

Our days would begin at the crack of dawn. *'The early bird catches the most worms'* Dad would say and even though we all had chores, Denny somehow ended up with the most, doing the worst jobs like cleaning the pigs' sties. Denny was slow in school. He had cracked feet, curly hair and the biggest hands I have ever seen on a boy.

At lunch time we would go down the hill, across the river and put on our shoes and socks that we took off on arrival at school. Then we'd climb up the other side of the hill and reach home for a hot, cooked lunch that Mom prepared. Depending on where Dad was working, we would also have to take his lunch to him before heading back to school by the time the bell rang. Despite all that, I did very well in school.

After school we would walk the long way home, past the Post Office to pick up any mail and use this time to play with our friends, but being careful to get home in good time. In those days, we were safe since all the adults looked out for the children. As children, we did NOT beg as this would mean a beating from the person we begged, then another when we got home. Trust me; we soon learnt to report anything we did on our way home because the beating would be more severe if a complaint was lodged before we volunteered.

Saturday evenings meant piano lessons with Miss Etha Campbell. I loved playing the piano but hated learning the notes, lines and spaces. I had so much to memorize when all I wanted to do was play and when I learnt to play, *do ra me fa so la ti do* I was thrilled!

Mrs. Campbell was old and often allowed us to get away with fooling around. I liked her. She always smelt so clean and was my complexion with the same type of hair. She was also so patient and soft spoken.

I remember going home one evening with the Post Mistress, Mrs. Blake. On reaching a bridge on a deserted part of the road, a man jumped out on us wielding a knife and demanding her handbag. I was six years old and in Grade One.

The man was a stranger and looked scary. His shirt was dirty and he had very ugly teeth with four at the front of his mouth missing. I was scared and hid behind Mrs. Blake. She gave him her bag and he told her if she reported it to the police he would kill her.

Unearthing the Diamond

As he walked away, he looked at me and grinned, shaking the knife. *"What are you looking at?"* he snarled. I remember clutching onto Mrs. Blake's skirt and shivering.

Of course she did report it to the police and a search or the area was made. Subsequently, he was found along the bank of the river and was caught! The next morning the police came to our home and I was excited because this police was dressed in uniform. In those days the police were not scary to children. As I spoke about the theft, the police began writing in his book. He asked me what had happened and I told him about how I left school and stopped by the Post office and waited for Mrs. Blake so that we could walk home together. I knew this was OK because she was going to see my grandmother. Finally I told about how we reached to the bridge and recounted all that happened. When he was done writing he asked me to put an *x* on a line he had drawn at the end of what he had written. I asked him why, he said because I could not write my name and that the x would be just fine.

Tamika Felina Pommells Williams

I proudly told him I could write my name and wrote Leyla Pommells but not before asking him to let me read what he had written first. He could not believe what I was saying - a six year old reading. I had once heard Uncle Laurel, the lawyer, telling Uncle Irvin to always read before signing his name. The police officer called Mama and Dad while I was reading. I was so proud.

I did not realize reading would've made them so happy and proud. I remember this as vivid as if it happened yesterday. As a small girl that was one of the moments where I was able to make them proud.

Several times, I needed to go to court with Mrs. Blake to give evidence until the case was settled. When it was over the thief whose name was Gabbidon was sentenced to five years at hard labour with twelve lashes.

Denny on the other hand struggled in school. He was not happy. He was overworked and I remembered him wetting his bed way past his twelfth birthday. This was always embarrassing for him as Dad would sternly tell him that Larry who was three years younger than him was not wetting his bed. This was no comfort to Denny who continued to wet his bed.

Pat left home shortly after he graduated from high school to join the police force. So this meant our workload at home had increased.

Our home was surrounded with flowers. We had dogs and my favourite was Tarzan, an Alsatian. He was a very smart dog. When Dad came home from the fields, he would call Tarzan who would rush obediently to him, waiting on a command. Dad would sit and use a machete to scrape a few burs from his khaki pants. That was all Tarzan needed to see as he would start biting the burs from Dad's pants till they were all gone.

Even the dog had a chore, or so it seemed.

We had a huge two sided gate at the entrance of our home to keep the dogs in, but looking back I think this was more to keep us in instead of the dogs.

In our home, Sunday dinners were special. We all had to dress up for dinner, and as a family, eat at a large table. We all ate with knives and forks. Dad insisted we sat and ate properly at the table and elbows on the table or playing at the table were definitely forbidden.

Another quote from him was: *"There's a time and place for everything"*.

There was one Sunday dinner that stuck in my mind and might have even saved my life. We sat to eat (no one could eat before Dad started) but somehow I always managed to finish eating before everybody else; maybe it was my way of staying a step ahead of Dad. You never knew what he would use as a lesson of life. I had no intention of sharing my dinner if one of my siblings asked. I finished first being careful to not look greedy. I sat there not looking at anyone since we weren't supposed to look at others while they ate - Dad said this was to *henka* or beg for food.

Suddenly, Dad asked if I would like some of his dinner.

My eyes lit up. "Yes Sar!" I replied.

"Come and take what you want," he said.

I took up my plate and went to the head of the table where he sat. Using my fork, I pointed to a piece of

Unearthing the Diamond

yellow yam, but what I really wanted was a piece of the chicken. I knew I could not take the best thing on his plate.

WHAP! Suddenly he hit me with his fork. I didn't understand why or what was happening and wanted to cry. I held back the tears while stealing a glance at my siblings. They were trying to hold back their laughter. I also knew if I cried it would mean a beating and if they laughed they would be beaten.

I stood there like a statue.

Mom broke the silence. "Haughton, you offered her food."

"Yes! But she is not hungry! She just had all her dinner. This is a lesson for her, for all of you," He pointed his knife at my siblings. "If you go out and even if you have had nothing to eat and you are offered food, say "'No thank you. I have just eaten.'", even if you are hungry. Do you hear me?"

"Yes Sar!"

"If you take food from anyone, take it home and give it to the dogs. No, better give it to your grandmother.

Tell her who gave it to you and she will decide if it can be given to the dogs or thrown away. I am envied in this community and people would want to hurt me but they can't. They can hurt me by hurting you. They will POISON you!"

Dad stared directly at me when he made that last statement and the fact that I could die by taking food from people, stuck in my head. He then put the piece of yellow yam in my plate and I went back to my seat and ate very slowly.

I hung my head in shame and I could hear him muttering under his breath. *"Cut and swallow your food hummmpff".*

That was one lesson I learnt and I learnt it well, especially with my siblings teasing me about it for what seemed like forever. Dad's favourite quote was: *"If you owned all the gold mines in the world and had no charikta (character) then you had nothing."* It meant nothing to me as a child but as I became a woman, the meaning became clear.

My Grandparents raised us to the best of their abilities and looking back on my life; I know that I

Unearthing the Diamond

was indeed blessed to have had them for my guardians. When I encountered the many struggles in my life, it was from their teachings and discipline that I have managed to survive. Dad's many quotes/parables have helped shaped my life and I now use those quotes today throughout my experiences in life. My husband and partner, Ian, reminds me so much of my grandfather and I am thankful to my aunt who decided to take us from our father and to her parents who did a fine job of raising us, despite the beatings. As I bring this chapter to a close, here is one of his quotes:

"What doesn't kill you will only make you stronger".

Tamika Felina Pommells Williams

Finding Dad

In 1974 I sat, and was successful, in the Common Entrance Examinations to enter high school. My Aunt Freddie came back for me. The night before we went back to Kingston, I overheard her speaking with Mama and Dad.

They strongly opposed the idea of me going away to high school in Kingston but Aunt Freddie said her daughter Audrey and I could keep each other company; furthermore, she wanted me since she was the one who had taken Denny, Larry and me to live with our grandparents in the first place.

Mama and Dad gave in. The next morning Cecile was so sad but I was happy! I loved Aunt Freddie; she always visited us in the country and often brought me beautiful dresses Audrey had outgrown. Cecile was older than me but because the dresses could only fit my sister, our grandmother put them in the wardrobe. I never got to wear them as we both had to wear the dresses Mama made for us.

Unearthing the Diamond

The drive to Kingston was long. It seemed we would never reach and when we did, there were so many vehicles on the roads. I knew my aunt lived in Harbour View and when I saw the community sign I was overjoyed. It was a housing scheme with the avenues named from things relating to the sea: Lagoon Avenue, Pearl Avenue, Reef Avenue, etc. My Aunt's home was on Pearl Avenue.

She had two children, Owen was an extremely tall young man and in fourth form at the high school I was going to attend. Audrey was in second form at St Hugh's High School for Girls. My Aunt's husband, Mr. Vincent Green was short and starting to lose hair on the top of his head. They owned a green Hillman Hunter motor car. Mr. Green wore glasses and it seemed Aunty Freddy towered over him. He didn't seem happy that I came to live with them but I didn't care because I knew Aunty Freddie wanted me to be there. The house had four bedrooms. I would share Audrey's bedroom which had twin beds.

The house had two bathrooms, one for Aunty Freddie and her husband and the other for us children. The kitchen and dining room were combined and located at the back of the house. The living room had settees made of wood. A black and white television and stereo were encased in polished wooden cases. There was a telephone on a side table in the living room but the best thing I saw was the piano. I decided that this was where I belonged and I would cook, clean and make myself useful so that they would not send me back to the country.

Excelsior High school was founded by Mr. W. Powell who was the principal when I first attended. He retired in my second year and a new principal by the name of Mr. Wong, took over. High school was definitely different from primary school. We had to move to the different classes where every subject had a different teacher. The school was big with separate bathrooms for girls, boys and staff. There was a huge auditorium, offices, labs, Home Economic rooms, Music Room with instruments, library, cafeteria, blocks for classrooms and a HUGE playing field.

Unearthing the Diamond

I joined the Girl Guides, Creative Dancing, Athletics and Sewing Groups. I had three friends to whom I was very close, Brendan Duncan, Grace Cole and Margaret Hopkins. We all enrolled in the same activities except for sewing as I was the only one from our group who enjoyed sewing (thanks to my grandmother).

I settled well into my first year of high school but by the end of the second year I wasn't happy. I missed and needed my mother terribly. I often lied to my classmates telling them my Mom was coming to look for me just for my birthday. I fabricated stories about the things we did when she came, but in truth, she never came. I just needed my mother's love, guidance and acceptance. Being a teenager in high school, I longed for my own mother. I was jealous of my cousin Audrey. I longed to have my own mom, someone to make me feel I wasn't abandoned and one who would give me the guidance I needed as a teenager - telling me about boys and most importantly to guide and help me to build my self confidence (which was non-existence).

Things weren't going as happy at my Aunt's home as I had initially imagined. I was still working as if I were in the country; cleaning the house and carport every Saturday while Audrey and Owen studied. Though I decided I wanted to be there, I was beginning to go through puberty and just wanted my own mother, someone to love me the way Aunty Freddy loved Audrey. I needed my OWN mother.

It seemed I was always trying to prove I was special. I couldn't understand why my mother would leave me. My mother had three children for my father: Denny, Larry and me. My father physically abused my mother so often that her parents and siblings decided to send her to England to her eldest sibling and brother Auzie, leaving us behind. Our Aunty Freddie took us from our dad and brought us to live with our grandparents and two other siblings who were already living there. Then, Aunty Freddie took me from my grandparents to live with her. What could I do? I know she left five of us but all I cared or worried about was how she left ME. I was desperate for attention and affection and needed my own family.

Unearthing the Diamond

One evening as I sat in front of the large wooden stereo in my Aunt's living-room I heard a lady on the radio (I think it was RJR), saying she could find loved ones. She supplied the address for the station. I quickly wrote it down, sending her a letter the following day by mail. This was in 1975. The lady's name was Mrs. Hazel Monteith.

After my Aunt took my brothers and me to live with our grandparents, our dad used to visit every Sunday. One Sunday he brought me a beautiful white doll with long flowing hair, I was ecstatic. My Dad picked me up and swung me around. My sister, Cecile, wanted to play with my doll and she took the doll from my hands. My Dad grabbed it away and said, "I don't want any monkey to play with my daughter's doll."

My grandfather was beside himself! He told my Dad to get off his land and never to come back. My grandfather also told him to take his: *"Alabaster baby and leave."* I was crushed. My Dad left and never visited us again. I knew my Dad was alive and in Jamaica. I knew he wanted me because I told myself he was ordered out of our lives. It made sense to respond to the radio ad saying it could find anyone and they did.

I didn't tell my aunt that I needed to find him. He had disappeared from our lives and if I could not be with my Mom I was hell bent on finding my Dad. A few days later my aunt got a telephone call from a woman who said she heard the programme on the radio looking for a Felix Pommells and he was her brother.

I asked myself, how was I going to get out of this one? I just owned up and told my aunt I wanted to find my Dad. She wanted to know why but I could not explain. How could I tell her I just wanted my Dad, someone who was mine and would make me feel wanted?

Aunty Sissy, my dad's sister, after hearing the information on the radio, made contact with him after she met me. He visited me at Aunty Freddie's home in Harbour View. Now I'd someone who was mine. He was *my* Dad. The next day Aunt Sissy came and met me and I loved her immediately! She was my flesh and blood and looked like how I remembered my Dad. That was the beginning of a relationship with my Dad that ended when he passed away April 13th 2003.

The first holiday from school came and he asked that I spend it with him. I was beside myself with joy. He picked me up in his van and we took the long drive to Burnt Savannah in St Elizabeth.

I remember thinking I wouldn't return to Kingston and that I would stay with *my* Dad. When we arrived, and to my horror, my Dad had two children living with him, Sydney and Stacey. His wife Carmen didn't want another woman's child in their home. It seemed physical abuse was also part of his modus operandi since for the short time I was there, he beat his wife several times. I knew this was no place for me and I withdrew into my shell.

But my Dad is an entire book in itself. I was able to spend some of my holidays with him but he wasn't mine. He was already living with his wife and two children and out at work, six days a week. I was left at home with the helper, brother, Sydney and sister,

Stacey, whenever I visited. I was empty inside. Searching for someone to love me and understand me. When my mother migrated to England I was about four-years-old and the bond between Denny, Larry and myself was, and still is, very strong.

My Grandfather was born on a slave plantation and now the tables were turned. He was now raising three children - whose father was white; even as children we knew we were treated differently. Larry, who was the baby, escaped the wrath of our Grandfather. He was the baby and was treated like their own. Denny was overworked and I was always scolded and beaten, while being told my colour and hair would get me nowhere in life. During this time, it was difficult for mixed children and so my pain at being abandoned by my mother was very intense.

At school I tried so hard to be liked but kept making things worse for myself as I was the only one in my class who didn't have a Mom or Dad; and though the other children never cared, it bothered me so much I often withdrew myself because I felt so different.

Unearthing the Diamond

I was good at drawing in school and often drew diagrams for classmates in Biology class. I felt needed and useful. I entered third form in September 1976. That was when I met Phillip. I thought I was in love. He was in fifth form. He was interested in me and cared. Finally, I had someone who cared about/for me. I didn't care that he wasn't my family. He was spending time with me whenever he could. In the evenings after school, we would sit on a concrete bench behind the library, under a Lignum Vitae tree. Here, we spoke about anything and everything. Phillip was tall & dark but not handsome; but made up for that by being kind and caring. He had pearly white teeth and was interested in everything I had to say. I told him about growing up without my Mom, being in the country with my Grandparents, moving back to Kingston to live with my Aunt and the emptiness in the pit of my stomach for not being with my Mom. I shared with him the problems I was having at home with my Aunt and how I felt about what I wanted to become when I grew up. I wanted to become a doctor so I could diagnose people's illnesses and make them better. Funnily, I actually used the word "diagnose" when I spoke with Phillip. Just seeing him made me happy and when he touched me, it felt so good, making me feel so special, so loved, so needed and important.

He enjoyed my company as much as I enjoyed his. One day, he mentioned I was different from what his friends thought of me since they thought of me as being *'stush'* (stuck up or better than others), proud and considering myself above them. This surprised me but did not bother me since Phillip knew differently. He knew I had my own set of problems living with my Aunt and being raised to not mix with everyone. Maybe there was some truth to what they had said.

I trusted Phillip completely!

Most of the times we would just hold hands; we never had sex but fondled each other and kissed. After all, he was my boyfriend. This went on for about four months until December 1976 - my fantasy about Phillip fell apart.

The bench behind the library under the Lignum Vitae tree was our daily meeting place. I was late that evening in particular. For some reason I had stayed behind in the Extension's sewing class. I had called my aunt to let her know I was still at school and in this class. I also knew she would call the school to verify this, but that was OK, I was in Sewing Class.

During the class, Phillip kept walking back and forth pass the door and each time he went by I would mouth "soon come" to him. When class was over, I rushed to our meeting place under the tree.

He was there waiting. He said it wasn't safe for us to sit there because the library was closed and it was getting dark, so we should go around to the first form blocks. It never dawned on me to say that it was better to stay where we were because at least the area was lighted. What was I worried about? Phillip was with me. I was safe.

I tried convincing myself but something inside me warned me to not go. It was getting dark and the first form blocks were all the way to the back of the school compound. We held hands and I went anyway.

Then there was a second warning.

When we reached the block, I noticed there was no padlock on the door on one of the classrooms. This was most unusual because the watchman always put padlocks on all the doors. Still, I put the feeling aside because I felt safe with Phillip being there with me. But the second he pushed the door open, my whole world crumbled. All I saw were MEN! Strange men! I looked at Phillip and the look on his face chilled me to the bones. I noticed in that instance that some of the 'men' were boys from my school and men I had never seen before.

Most of the boys in uniform were on the football team. I saw a boy, who was a CHRISTIAN. I searched his eyes, begging silently for his help. He just hung his head and looked away. I was DEAD! That is all I could think now! They were going to kill me, they had to. They began pulling at me and I screamed for *PHILLIP!!*

"You think you better than me?" one shouted! I tried for the door but could not move. Now, panic set in. Dear God, why can't I move? How can I not move?

Unearthing the Diamond

One of the men had a piece of pitch pine plank of wood in his hand! He used it to hit the desk. "You fucker you, we going to fuck you till we bring you down to size. All ah unno red kin gal tink unno betta dan people."

My mind was telling me to scream, run, call out for help but my mouth could not open and my feet felt glued to the ground. It was as if I was having an 'out-of-body' experience – I was watching all this happening to me. *For God's sake why can't I move?* I stood there shivering, the tears falling down my face.

Suddenly, Phillip said, "Me first! Me first!"

I was now able to move and ran to the back of the classroom screaming *HELP! HELP!* I am still unsure if any words came from my mouth or if I only thought them. I felt hands as they caught me and dragged me across a desk and held me down. I don't know how my underwear came off. They were holding my shoulders, my hands, my legs. *Good God! Dear Lord kill me, please take my life! Don't let this happen to me! Kill me first!* I thought as I closed my eyes. No answer came from God! No help from anyone. A sudden thrust and Phillip was in me. He kept cursing me, spitting out the words at me: "Four months! Four whole months and you couldn't give me! Now me teck it. You slut! You dog! Only a slut has so many bulls. You fucking slut dog!"

Next, was the man with the plank - he had dreadlocks. He pulled me away from the other men who were holding me down and just threw me around like a rag doll. "Let go off her Bumboclatt! Let har go! Di gal need some bumboclatt lick!" With that he hit me so hard with the plank; it broke across my left thigh. I screamed from within my belly and this made him even madder.

"Gal you want me kill you tonight? Shut you fucking mouth!" I whimpered like a helpless child. He hit me again with the piece of wood and all I could smell was the pitch pine. "You want a fuck you wid dis piece a hood dutty gal?" He said, pointing it in my face.

'God, PLEASE make me die!' I found myself thinking. *If they don't kill me and God won't kill me, then my aunt would kill me for sure. Somehow, I am going to*

Unearthing the Diamond

die tonight! This was worse than a nightmare! At least I would've awakened from a scary nightmare, I figured. Here, I was alive and wanted to die but wasn't.

Delroy was Phillip's best friend. He grabbed the piece of wood from the man and said, "You making too much noise and a nuff a we to go! Come on man, just fuck de rass gal." The man hissed his teeth and held me back. I closed my eyes against what was happening. I tried to leave my mind but for some strange reason, my mind decided it wanted to hear, to feel and instead, recorded everything that was happening. I had no escape - not even from my own mind.

The man entered me. "A long time me a watch you, you fucker you. You tink you nice? Mek me see you walk and gallang like you a sumaddy now." They were back to holding me down. *HELP! HELP! Anybody Please HELP ME!* I screamed! However, within, silently.

I stopped counting after the 13th one entered me. With each one, I just kept wishing I was dead. At one point I opened my eyes and saw "the Christian" between my legs. He was about to enter me. I whispered, "Please don't hurt me; don't do this I beg you, you are a Christian." He didn't and stepped away. They started to tease him and he held his head down as he walked away.

When they were all done, Phillip tossed my underwear at me. "Put on your drawers! Go ah yuh yard!" With them snickering and muttering to themselves, they left me alone. I rolled off the desk, sat on the floor, pulled my knees up to my chest and cried. *What have I done? How could I have allowed this to happen? Why am I still alive? How did I survive this?*

I staggered to my feet. I was as weak as a rat and my knees were wobbly. My hips were sore and my entire body ached. Somehow they were careful to not hit me in my face or on my hands. I was now dirty and bloody, not just from my clothes but I was so dirty and I could not get clean. I kept thinking over and over. *Why hadn't I died? How come?* I just sat there hugging myself, *How can I ever keep this secret?* I was sure everyone would know just by looking at me that I was soiled for life!

I could not go home, not like this and I hid like a thief, making my way off the school compound in the shadows. I could not afford for anyone to see me as I boarded the Number 27 Bus and went down Mountain View Avenue, then taking the Number 2 Bus to Harbour View.

I was smelly and so dirty and I felt like everyone on the buses must have known what had happened to me. I went home and headed straight for the bathroom, sitting in the shower, allowing it to fall on me like rain. No matter how much I washed myself I could not get clean or wash the scenes that were in my mind. I told no one. While in the shower I could hear them calling my name over and over again. The name my parents gave me, the name I loved so much was now a dirty name. I hated it. Leyla you fucking slut over and over.

Suddenly my aunt called out "LEYLA! Are you OK in there?"

I whispered, "Just washing my hair aunt Freddie."

That was the first night I ever had a sleepless night. I lay in the bed in a fetal position hugging my knees and reliving every horrible moment. My eyes were swollen and I could hardly breathe. *I did not die! No one has to know. I can go on*, I convinced myself.

The following day was school. I thought I could go, but, I couldn't. I took the bus, got off in Downtown, Kingston and just walked around (albeit in my uniform) until it was time to go home. I did this for the following week. I could not face the school, my friends or any of the boys.

Christmas holidays were coming up and I would be over this by January, I thought. The holidays came and instead of getting better I was becoming worse. I wanted to kill myself but was so scared, too coward to even kill myself. Along with being called and treated like a slut dog, I was also a coward - Leyla, the coward dog!

I locked myself in the room I shared with Audrey and she didn't like me anymore because I spent the holidays sleeping. She thought I was acting strange. She must've been tired of hearing me cry at nights or just the pitiful way I was, especially in comparison to how I was before, where I used to be singing, dancing and TALKING. Now, suddenly, NOTHING!

Aunty Freddie wasn't concerned. As far as she knew I wasn't acting up, getting into any trouble and just wanted to stay home. I was no longer a cause for any quarrels between her and Mr. Green; whatever they wanted me to do was done straight away with no arguments. I must have seemed like the perfect child and if she suspected that things were terribly amiss with me, she never asked

January 1977 came and with it the first day back at school. I knew I had to attend and thought I would be perfect if I stayed around a crowd and away from Phillip and his friends.

The first day of school was General Assembly and we stood in class groups. I thought I was safe and went with my class. Suddenly, I felt I was being watched and turned around to see Delroy and Phillip there.

"If you ever breathe a word of what happened to anyone," whispered Phillip.

This time my feet worked and I ran away, with everyone looking at me, wondering if I was insane. I stopped at the bathroom which was attached to the 3rd Form block where my class was. One of my teachers, Mrs. Reid, had chased after me and was now in the bathroom with me. She found me huddled in a corner on the floor beside a basin. I was crying and holding my knees to my stomach just shaking myself. She knelt and hugged me and I heard myself telling her EVERYTHING that had happened.

"Are you sure?" She asked.

"Yes! Yes! YES! Just ask Phillip and Delroy," I said.

I asked her to not tell anyone because I didn't want them to hurt me. She said it was ok and she would help me get through this and I should trust her but I doubted her; the last time I trusted someone look what that got me. She stayed with me and took me back to class which had begun by the time we got there. All eyes were on me and I felt everyone knew. Everyone knew the DOG I was.

Unearthing the Diamond

The next morning Mrs. Reid called me and told me she had spoken to her husband who was a lawyer and he thought we should go to the principal.

"NOOOOO I can't." I cried. "He is a man; you promised you wouldn't tell anyone!"

"Trust me," she said.

"Nooo, please don't let me tell Mr. Wong!"

"I will be there with you," she said, "I will be there with you; you have to trust me, I want to help you. This is the only way."

So we both went to the office. We entered the office and I was scared. Mr. Wong told me to have a seat. I sat, holding my hands in my lap. I could feel my heartbeat in my throat and the room was so quiet.

"Come on Leyla, tell Mr. Wong what you told me." said Mrs. Reid. I lowered my head.

"It's alright," he said, "you won't get in trouble but I need to hear it from you."

I began to cry but finally through my sobs I told him, not in as much detail as I had told Mrs. Reid. When I was finished he said: "Now Leyla, I think you made this all up because you heard about what happened to Sharon during the last week of the Christmas Term. Some men, NOT members of this establishment, raped her and left her unconscious. She was found by the watch man. I can understand your need for attention but making up a story like this to draw attention to yourself; can only bring harm to this school."

What was he talking about? I was not at school the last week and no one told me about Sharon. All I knew was what had happened to me. He was so sure about how he said I had made it all up, that I could not even respond. I just crawled back into my shell. The tears fell freely now. I made one last attempt to be heard.

"Ask Phillip and Delroy," I whispered. "Check the register I wasn't at school the last week I could not face anyone ask them!" I began to shout. "You have to believe me! You have to! I am telling the truth! Why would I make this up about myself?"

"Please be quiet in this office young lady. Do you realize what you are saying? This school has a fine reputation; this fabrication can do nothing but harm it. Do you realize that? Do you?"

"Ask them PLEASE! I know I am not lying. I didn't imagine it, ask them!"

"Have you told anyone besides Mrs. Reid?"

"No," I replied.

"You say this happened the week before school gave holidays and you are now only speaking about it! You told NO ONE? How can I believe you? That's it I am calling your guardian. Go back to your class and wait till I send for you."

I looked at Mrs. Reid. I was totally broken as I said, "You promised me it would be alright. You promised me you would keep my secret. You promised."

She calmly stated. "I did. You are the one who told Mr. Wong."

I felt betrayed and hung my head as I returned to my class. The walk was painful. *How could I face my classmates? When was this ever going to end?* I didn't hear a word said in class. I was distraught. Now I had to face my aunt. If only I had told her. If only I had told someone, I kept saying to myself.

I knew how upset she would be. She was a teacher and would have to leave her class, her school, to come to a meeting with the principal and hear about what had happened to me. She would know I must be in some serious trouble and I just wanted to run away before she got there, but there was nowhere to go, nobody to turn to. I was all alone.

It seemed like hours went by and finally I was summoned to the office. My Geography teacher told me in front of the class to pack up my belongings and take them with me to the Principal's Office. *Good Lord I was being kicked out of school for something I didn't do. I was the one RAPED. How can I be kicked out? How can I?*

I walked away from my class hearing the whispers but didn't look back. I wished for lightening to strike me dead or the ground to open and swallow me, anything but this. I couldn't survive this I just couldn't.

Unearthing the Diamond

Finally I got to the office and my aunt was sitting there. She looked so small and was crying. I looked at her with the tears running down her face.

"I'm sorry," I said and for the first time in my life I saw fear on her face. She too didn't know what to do. Mr. Wong broke the silence and said, "You will need to find a school for her. Her grades are good so I am sure you will have no trouble placing her.

I'd never seen my Aunt cry before and have no idea what the Principal said to her, but I guessed from her tears she was having a hard time comprehending the situation as all her good intentions seemed to backfire in her face. She wanted a better life for my brothers and me and the amount of pain was now unbearable. I felt sorry for her since her plans that I'd be a companion for her daughter was not working out. I can imagine the fear she must've felt when she realized she had to inform my Grandfather about me being kicked out of high school and being brutally gang raped.

Finally Aunty Freddie got up, shook hands and told me to come with her as we were going home.

She didn't seem angry at me and my heart skipped a beat. "She believes me," I said to myself. Finally, someone believed me. She was so quiet as we headed for her car and the drive home was silent. I was scared to speak. I didn't know what to say.

The second we got out of the car she spoke. "How am I supposed to find another school for you?"

I hung my head in shame, the fear in my stomach returning.

"Do you realize what you have done? Who told you about the girl, Sharon, who was raped?"

"No one," I whispered, then after a while added, "Mr. Wong."

"How could you make this up? To get my attention? Well now you have it! The shame! How am I to hold up my head at church, in the community? What were you thinking? After all I have done for you? Taking you into my home, treating you like my own daughter. This is how you repay me? What am I supposed to tell Vin (her husband)? Answer me! What am I supposed to tell him?"

Unearthing the Diamond

I didn't know it was possible to feel any worse but I did. Her pain was as much as mine. I knew she knew that I was telling the truth but she could not bring herself to believe and so chose to protect herself as best as she could. She was crying openly now as if asking me to forgive her but I needed someone to hold me, fight for me, and protect me. I was more alone than I had ever felt.

She walked quietly into the house and headed for Audrey's room. She stripped the bed, taking my clothes and belongings out of the room. I didn't know what to do. She threw my things on the bed in the guest room. I felt my spirit sink further. I was no good; she had to protect her daughter from me. I was contaminated and worse contagious. She was afraid the same might happen to her daughter I thought to myself.

When she walked away I locked the door and crawled into the bed, lay on my clothes, feeling sorry for myself. I was nobody's child. No one wanted me, cared about me, believed me or fought for me.

That evening when her husband came home from work he was so upset. He didn't say a word as she spoke to him and his silence hurt more than if he was shouting. She cooked dinner and no one called me to the table, though I wasn't hungry anyway, but it still hurt. I don't know what explanation was given to Audrey when she asked why I was no longer in her room. I didn't care.

That night I heard my aunt and her husband quarrelling. He said I had to leave. He asked her why she had saddled them with caring for me and now this. Then he asked her a question I was asking myself over and over, "Where is her mother?" I put my pillow over my ears and cried myself to sleep.

I stayed home all alone that week as I had no school to attend. By the weekend, she told me I was to go to the dressmakers with her to fit my new uniform. I didn't dare ask which school I was going and at the dressmakers I was fitted with a green uniform. The uniform was for Vauxhall Secondary School. The school had a bad reputation and I knew that as young as I was, it was a demotion. I was moving from

Unearthing the Diamond

a prestigious high school to a secondary school and it seemed I would spend the rest of my life being punished for something done to me.

I didn't ask for this! NOONE would!

My family was the talk of the community. I could not stand being called by the name I loved so much, the name my parent's gave me at birth. I hated who I was and the sound of anyone calling me Leyla made my stomach turn. The memories stayed with me and just to call me Leyla put me right back in that classroom.

I began calling myself Tamika and only answered to Leyla at school when the daily register was marked or when my family called me. Going to this new school was not easy. Somehow word got out that I used to attend Excelsior High School and everyone knew what happened. I felt like a target, so I started staying in groups even if no one was speaking to me.

After the first month, I accepted the fact that I was here to stay and questions began coming to mind. What would happen if I sat and passed another exam from this school and passed to go back to Excelsior?

But that would never happen since my grades DROPPED!

I started playing netball. Then one day a girl from Excelsior by the name of Sylmadel Coke came to visit me at Vauxhall. It felt strange seeing her on the netball court wearing the uniform I once proudly wore. She heard I was now enrolled in Vauxhall and came to let me know she believed me and thought the school had done me wrong. She also told me that the same day I was expelled from school both Phillip and Delroy were transferred to a prominent high school, Wolmers Boys High School. I was devastated! *They were transferred* to a high school and here I was in a secondary school!

For the first time I was angry and on my way home from school I stopped at the top of my road and spoke with a Rastaman named Andrew. No one else would be seen with me and the Rastas (in the 70s) were outcasts, so I felt I found a kindred spirit. I told Andrew all that happened and how I found out the boys were transferred. He was livid! He said he would take me to school the next day on his bike but we would first pay a visit to Wolmers High School.

The next morning I got on Andrew's bike and headed for Wolmers. As we rode into the school I spotted Phillip and Delroy sitting under a tree in front of the school. I pointed them out to Andrew. We rode over and I wasn't scared to look at them. Andrew got off his bike, Phillip got up while Delroy just sat there. They were both scared.

Andrew spoke first: "Unno want a man shoot unno! Is wha dat unno doing to the little princess?" He said as he walked up to Phillip's face.

Phillip stuttered, "Nothing like that happened. She was my girl. I swear nothing like that happened."

Delroy hung his head. I could not believe my ears. Now a crowd was gathering and someone mentioned calling the police. Andrew said: "Come let's go." (He had locks and if the police came he would be arrested no questions asked, plus my Aunt). We rode away and he dropped me at school, asking me to stop by his home that evening as he was going to speak to some of his friends. That was the night I met Ian. Visiting and speaking to Ian, Andrew and their friends made me feel so alive. Most of our discussions were about Black people, our struggles, slavery and emancipating ourselves.

Finally, I belonged to a group of people who believed me and thought I was worth something. Yes they were considered rejects of society but I did not wish to be a part of a society that would not protect a girl, who would force a woman to take a child from school for fear of the school's reputation. I felt like a coward; but now as I write I clearly I see the cowards in my life and I am a STRONG woman and must have been a strong girl to have survived all I was forced to deal with and still come out with my sanity. Writing this book is the first part of therapy I have, since that incident more than thirty years ago.

THE COWARDS My Mom - for running off and leaving her five children at the mercy of others.

The men who raped me - All cowards! Phillip - especially Phillip! Trust me, he had said that he'd won my trust and abused it along with me. Mrs.

Unearthing the Diamond

Reid! - Oh Mrs. Reid, my English teacher. I survived it all without your help and guess what I am a teacher. Who would've thought? Mr. Wong - You chose to not believe me but you did BELIEVE! You were the biggest coward of all, forcing my Aunt to take me out of your school, telling her I was not expelled but that she had to find me a new school to protect yourself. But as a teacher and a principal myself I have learned that the students make the school; not the teachers or the parents but the students. You were not to blame for what happened to me, but I blamed you for how you didn't help me and my family.

Those are the cowards and as for my Aunt, I love her. She did the best she could and somehow I knew that day she believed me. Many years later she would visit my home and apologize to me and my husband. She thanked him for caring for me when no one else would!

In June 1977, my Aunt heard that I had gone to Ian's home. That was the straw that broke the camel's back. She beat me and told me to leave with nothing but the clothes on my back. I was kicked out of her home!

With nowhere to go, I went to Ian, who had no need of a troubled 15 year-old girl. He took me to his mom, asking her to allow me to live with her since Judy (his sister) and I used to attend the same school. I could use her clothes till he got paid to get me some. But his mother would have none of it. She had her hands full with raising her last two girls with help from only Ian and another sister. She asked about my family; but eventually, she said NO!

Ian was determined to help me and decided he wasn't going to allow me to return to my Aunt's. He said I had been through too much for one so young and so he took me on his bike and took me to his home. That night I slept in Ian's bed - in his underwear and shirt.

I would've done anything for him. He wouldn't touch me because he had a woman and I was a little girl. He had saved me and was even allowing me to wear his clothes - even his underwear. This was the man for me.

He could not afford to send me back to school on his salary as he was a single man living in a one-room and helping his mom to school his sisters, as well as a dad who was ill. He taught me everything he knew. He encouraged me to read, read and read. I remember him saying that, I could travel the world by reading and imagining and so I read every book I could get my hands on. With his help, I managed to educate myself. He always told me I needed to build my self confidence and self esteem.

Once, he told me his goal in life was that if he died, he would like to know I could take care of myself. He said I could be ANYTHING I wanted, the sky was the limit. I hung onto his every word and I loved him with all my soul!

NOTE: (April 23, 2009) In late 2008 I found Sylmadel Coke on Facebook. I could not believe it. She remembered me and has been searching for me for over thirty years. We spoke about her grandmother and she informed me that her grandmother was asking about me even on her death bed. A few days ago I saw Sylmadel on Facebook and told her I had finally decided to give myself the therapy I so desperately needed and was doing this by way of writing a book about my life. I asked if she cared to see what I had written. She eagerly said I should send it, so I copied and sent the first two chapters I had completed.

The next day I got the following messages from her on Facebook: *"Once my emotional reaction has lessened a bit, I will give you a more critical reading of the book. If it is ok with you, I would like to make a few comments and ask a few questions that will bring out more. There are also some bits of things that I want to tell you. I realize that this is your first "therapy" but since you want to publish it, it also has to be a good read. Tell Ian I said Thank you. I have to stop now".*

Second message from Sylmadel: *"I spent the day at work weeping inside like a lost puppy. The images overwhelm me. I never anticipated that when this* *moment came, you would have to be strengthening me. Thank you. I am weak again. A teenage girl again. Helpless again. I used to imagine that when we connected again, I would be the one giving you strength. I do not think for one moment that my reaction to your experience could even come close to what you have lived through/with. Sis, it just hurts to see it in writing, and becoming a helpless, wandering teenager again. I had no idea I would feel like this. I want to say sorry, yet in a deeper human way, I am not".*

Her third message: *"I stayed in bed for most of the day and read.... Again and again. I cried. I prayed. I hate. I rage. I read to a friend. She cried for you and me. She cried for herself. I cannot claim to love another woman as purely as I love you. I am not ashamed. I carried that one horrific moment with me for thirty years. Thirty years of injustice. Thirty years of silence. Thirty years of pain. It has taken thirty years for this flower to bloom for me. Thank you".*

My response: *"My sweet Sylmadel. I didn't mean for you to cry, hate or feel rage. I just wanted to share* *what I am doing to help myself with you because I Do love you and care about you. It has been 32 years and 4 months. It took me this long because I had locked it all away for so long. That was the only way I would have been able to survive. I have so many blessings in my life! I decided to NOT allow the cowards to dictate my happiness! In a way my life was always incomplete. The day I wrote Chapter Two, I sat in my garden for hours and literally opened that horrid door and looked in. I don't know if this feeling of fear or helplessness will ever go away but I am who I am. I have been blessed with a man who loves me COMPLETELY and has been my strength. As a matter of fact, I opened the door not just for me but for him. I only regret that your grandma passed away before knowing I survived but I know that she is an angel with wings.*

In my heart I know that she knows.

My life has been from one extreme to the next, either horrid experiences or great ones but I have learnt lessons from them all. I will publish this book. I am NOT afraid. Thank you for loving me all these years

Unearthing the Diamond

and for coming to visit me at Vauxhall, You were the only one who dared to come see me, the only one who cared. When I am done with this book you will be thanked. I love you my sister. I love you.

Please tell your friend I appreciate her tears but she should really pray for the ignorant cowards. I cannot begin to imagine the torment they must feel and if they sleep well at nights. Somewhere, even before they take their last breath, they will remember and ask God to forgive them for all they did to me and my family. My only true friend from school was you. I have forgiven all of them.

I am blessed. l- o- v- e is only four letters but they say EVERYTHING. I have love. I love you."

Tamika Felina Pommells Williams

On The Move

Living with Ian was different. I was free! He went to work while I stayed with his friend's partner, Dawn, and her two children, Tracey and Trecia. I used the time to read and sleep. There was nothing else to do. I was 15 years old with no family or friend and NO television! I would also make sure dinner was ready when he came home.

This went on for about a month until one Friday Ian got a call at work from his landlady (who had rented him a room in her home). She told him that the police came by with a warrant for his arrest. He was being charged with kidnapping! Who did he kidnap? I could not believe it. After living openly with Ian for over a month, less than a block away from my Aunt's home, she suddenly decided to report me to the police as being kidnapped.

I was scared, upset and angry.

I could NOT go back to the life I had. No more beatings, no more being told I was worthless and no good. We had struggled for that month but it was my first taste of freedom. I would NEVER go back.

Ian was a Rastaman. The police would not listen to him. He had never been in trouble with the law and his only crime was trying to help and provide for me a place where I was safe.

We decided to run for it and after dodging the police for about a week we packed all our things and fled before dawn to St. Mary. We had no family or friends in St. Mary but Ian's friend had family and so we all moved there. Six of us – Mackie; Mackie was Ian's friend and he was the reason we moved to St Mary. He was the father of the two girls Trecia and Tracey and Dawn's partner. A mutual friend named Jahwho took us one night in his truck to Broadgate in St Mary.

Dawn and Mackie, their two daughters, Ian and me. We rented two rooms. Two beds were placed in one room separated by two brown polka dot shower curtains and the two girls shared the front room. The house was situated on the side of the main road where we could hear every vehicle passing by. The six of us occupied one section of the house while two other families occupied the rest. This was my first experience living in a tenement yard. There was electricity but NO running water. We had to go across the road and down to the river to wash and carry water to cook and boil for drinking.

I desperately wanted to become pregnant. Ian kept telling me to wait because I was too young and needed to become educated. It was bad enough that the police were looking for me/us, so he couldn't afford for me to be pregnant at fifteen. I needed to find a way to keep him, this had to last I thought to myself and I WAS going to have his baby. About two months later I did become pregnant but miscarried. I was devastated.

Broad Gate was not for us. There was nowhere to look but directly at the mountains just standing there boxing us in and the situation of living the six of us in such a small space became problematic for us and so we decided to move again. Before deciding on where to move to this time, Ian sat me down one evening on a hassock and he knelt in front of me.

Unearthing the Diamond

"Tamika," he said, "I know I promised to make things better for you but without a job and the plan to move and the uncertainty of the future I think it's best for you to go back to your Dad in St Elizabeth." He must have seen the fear in my eyes because he hurriedly added, "Not for a long time Tamika only till things get better and I will come back for you."

Tears sprang to my eyes. I saw him leaving me and thought this was an excuse to get rid of me. Out of desperation I found myself quoting from the Bible, the tears streaming down my face: "Entreat me not to leave thee, or to return from following after thee. For whether thou goest I will go and where thou lodgest I will lodge. Thy people shall be my people and thy God my God."

Ian just looked at me. He hugged me and said it was going to be a hard journey and we might meet a lot of sufferation but together we would be able to face anything. The look on his face and the tenderness in his eyes said he wasn't looking for a way out, he wasn't abandoning me, and he was just concerned and wanted to spare me the suffering he knew that lay ahead. I was prepared to take whatever suffering as long as he stayed with me. This time we had to go where one of us had family and so we chose to go to Portland because Ian's Dad had given him a piece of land there and he had family there.

We lived in St Mary for five months and on December 31st 1977 we moved to Portland. We had rented a little house above The Blue Lagoon and we thought this was a safe place to live. Most importantly we had the famous Blue Lagoon adjacent to the property we were renting as well as the OCEAN. Ian LOVED the ocean. We could go swimming in it whenever we liked. It was less than a minute's walk away. *OHHHHHH I remember the Spring running into the Blue Lagoon, icy cold but it felt soooo good.*

Leaving St Mary behind, meant we were now totally on our own and the relationship between Mackie, his family and us soured. They decided to go back to Kingston and we headed to Fairy Hill, Portland. To this day neither Ian nor I ever ran into any of them.

Unearthing the Diamond

Ian had lost his job as an accountant and now we were in a parish where he had some extended family but we were pretty much strangers in a strange land.

Portland is the most beautiful parish on the island - rain fell EVERY DAY! When we moved there it rained non-stop for two whole weeks. We had never seen that much rain in our lives and we spent quality time settling in and enjoying the rain and each other.

One day stands out in my mind.

We had run out of kerosene oil for the stove and needed to cook, so I gathered some wood and started a fire, putting on the pot and began to cook our dinner. While the pot was boiling, it began to rain. I ran for a piece of aluminum zinc and covered the pot. *Yeah I felt so good I came up with an idea which the rain could not stop dinner from being cooked.*

Suddenly a stream of water started to come around the corner. I watched helpless and it washed the fire completely from under the pot leaving the stones standing with the pot on them.

"IAN COME LOOK!" I began to cry. Ian came and burst out in laughter. I was crying because I was hungry and he thought this was funny.

He held me and said, "It's ok Tamika, its ok. I will remake the fire inside and finish the dinner."

Now, I smiled too at the memory of the rain washing away the fire under my pot.

Portland is by far the most beautiful parish on the island. It was the last parish to stop working as slaves and the people are what some would call small minded and simple. Most of the young people at the time had only one or two opportunities to better themselves. Working on a cruise ship, prostitution or working in a small bank. There was never enough space for the applicants and it was a privilege to be working in either field.

Ian had quit his job as an accountant and we had no way of earning money. He walked every street in Port Antonio looking for a job. No one would hire him. He was more than qualified but he had locks and so was always refused employment because of his beliefs and hair. Every day he would leave me at home and go in search of a job or something for us to eat.

One evening he came home and told me he got a job. I was overjoyed. I jumped on him with my legs wrapped around his waist and hugged and kissed him. I was so childish and expressed my delight at him getting a job. When he put me down I asked where the job was, what kind of job it was and should I prepare clothes for him to wear? That's when he told me it was in the construction of a road.

A road was being built and they needed labourers. Labourers would use shovels in order to spread marl but Ian had NO shovel and I asked him how was he going to do it? He was an accountant for Christ's sake. How could he help build a road? He said: *"My dad told me when I was a boy, 'You born name ram, knife have to touch your seed"*. I looked at him not understanding what he said. He said, *"I am the head of the house and I will do what I have to do to provide for you. I have walked everywhere and no one will hire me. This is the only way."*

The next morning he got up had a cup of tea and went to work. That was such a long day. When he finally got home he looked so exhausted but never complained. His hands hurt and I was so sad for him. He told me that because he had no shovel he had to pick up the marl heads and throw them in front of the roller and he did that all day. With no money he worked all day with nothing to eat and was so tired! He did this for two weeks, leaving home each morning begging a lift to work, jumping on the back of moving trucks and doing the same to get home. I took food from a nearby shop and made sure dinner was ready whenever he got home. When he got paid, we would pay the bills at the shop, the rent and buy some food. Soon the money was gone.

I felt I was a burden to him because he had lost his accounting job because of me and now he had to be working so hard, away from his friends and family and taking care of me. I vowed to make sure he would never regret it.

Before we moved from St Mary to Portland, I had a toothache one day. It hurt for days. We went to a dentist who said we had to pay to extract the tooth; Ian went to his boss and asked for an advance on his pay so that he could pay the dentist.

His boss refused. Ian told him he needed the money because I was in pain and when he refused yet again Ian got so upset. He told his boss that he had been working as their accountant for over seven years and had never asked them for anything, and now that he needed money to have my tooth extracted they would not assist. All I heard was when Ian said: "Pay me up. You won't advance me some of my pay? I quit! Pay me up NOW!"

His boss was shocked but he quickly went to his office and wrote a cheque to Ian who cashed it at the bank and took me to have my tooth extracted. He did that for me. No one ever, in all my life, sacrificed anything for me. He never mentioned that to me even when I would say we were suffering because of me, he never blamed me and always went out to find food or any odd jobs he could find to provide for the both of us.

Tamika Felina Pommells Williams

Living in Portland on our own forced me to grow up much faster than a typical teenager. I was now living in a situation where I was a housewife at the age of sixteen. I loved the freedom but was often scared about how we would survive the next day. We often scouted the bushes for yams and I taught Ian how to dig them and how to tell if they were ready for eating, this I learnt while growing up on the farm with Dad. The house we rented above the famous Blue Lagoon was cultivated with coconuts.

We were sure we had found a way to stay alive. Each morning we would climb the hill and head for the coconut plantation and ate and drank jelly coconuts till our bellies were filled. We would take some back home with us to eat for lunch or dinner. After a week of eating nothing but coconuts we both became sick to our stomachs from eating too many coconuts. We had eaten enough. Next, we had an apple tree, right by the house. When it finally bore apples, that was our source of food, I ate apples in every which way - stewed apples, apple juice and ripe apples. And of course, soon our bodies rejected apples.

Unearthing the Diamond

Close to the house, on a property adjacent to where we lived, there was a farm of bananas and avocados. We would take turns to make sure the owner wasn't coming whenever we stole a bunch of bananas. When it was avocado season, we would get up at the crack of dawn to search for avocados which had fallen from the trees. Sometimes we were lucky and found a ripe one which was half eaten by rats or cats and would peel away the eaten portion, taking home the rest.

How I loved breadfruit season. It meant we could get a staple and for free. It was being given away and all they needed was a fire to roast them. I still don't know how we survived Portland but my love, my darling, my husband, my life; we did.

Then out of sheer desperation, we decided to go up in the hills of May Mountains and start a farm. A friend we met while we lived in Portland was a farmer in May Mountain. He said we could just go and clear a piece of land and farm it. We would walk each morning for at least four miles to get to our farm up in the mountains. The first half of the walk led us past San San Development. The richer persons lived in this area. By the time we got to our farm, I was usually wiped out from the walk.

Ian and I cleared a piece of land and started tilling it to cultivate for food. We started playing with the idea of living in the hills. I was so young but was determined to survive with Ian. Armed with our machetes we would chop down huge twenty and thirty feet bamboo and carried them to where our farm was located. We were going to make our home and this process of cutting the bamboo and carrying it to our farm was a long and tedious job. Finally, we built our one room bamboo house. The roof, floor, windows, doors and walls all made of bamboo. We purchased some supplies and decided we would move to the mountain. This was how we passed the time each day - walking four miles to get to our farm then walking back the same distance to get home in the evenings.

One night on our way home we were each carrying breadfruits tied in a bundle on our heads and I was tired. About three quarters of a mile from home I couldn't carry my load any further. I just took them off my head set them down and started crying, telling Ian this life was too hard. I had reached my breaking point. I could not carry the breadfruit any further. I felt ashamed that I had given up but I was so tired and really couldn't go any further. I felt so exhausted. I wasn't even sure I could walk the rest of the way home. Ian calmly took the load off his head and hid mine in the bushes and said it was ok.

We went home, with Ian carrying his load of breadfruits.

When we got home, he put his load down then walked back to where he hid my load and took that home too. All this time I was crying he never got upset with me. He only said we needed all the breadfruits for food so he could not leave them; he also said we couldn't live in the mountains. He said if one of us became ill, it would be too much to get to the hospital and that it was no place to raise a child.

It was difficult living with no one else to depend on but Ian. He was my everything. I needed to hold on to him but was too young to be married; and to top it all, Ian didn't want to be married. I decided I needed to get pregnant and have his baby. I convinced myself that this would force him to stay with me and I would have someone else to love and be loved. But It seems nothing I wanted came easily.

We didn't use birth control and still I didn't become pregnant. I felt so incomplete. I started feeling desperate and often went to bed crying and begging God to make me pregnant.

Even so, we somehow managed to survive with me being totally dependent on Ian. By now I had changed my appearance and had grown dreadlocks. My hair grew quickly and soon my locks were even longer than Ian's. I looked older with dreadlocks. To this day, Ian insists that it is the most beautiful he has ever seen me.

However, I didn't just stay at home waiting on Ian to provide for me. I knitted baby's sweaters, hats and booties and these Ian would take out and sell. I taught Ian to make floor mats from Bull rushes which he also sold. The craziest thing I did was to put up a sign at our gate which said 'Dressmaking done here'. I didn't have a sewing machine but I took

Unearthing the Diamond

my time and sew neatly. My first customer was a woman named Gene, who ordered a white one piece jumper to wear to a wedding. I took her measurements on the veranda and sewed the outfit day and night until it was done. We had no electricity at the time, so at nights I sew by the Home Sweet Home kerosene lamp. When the woman picked up her outfit she fitted it and I was so proud. I was only 16 at this point.

In December 1978 I was working as a domestic helper for a one-hand man named Horatio. He was married to one of the most beautiful white woman I have ever seen, her name was Geovannah. They operated a restaurant at the Blue Lagoon.

One morning I showed up for work and he told me I should go under the cellar of the house to count the pups his dog had the night before. I was scared to because it was a tiny opening for a door and it was completely dark under there. But I had no choice. I needed the job.

Gingerly, I knelt on my knees and peered in through the opening. I had a flash light in one hand. The stench was overwhelming and I gagged a couple of times. My hands and knees were dirty from crawling around in the cellar searching for the dog and her pups. I heard her growling. Then I felt something soft in my hand. I had placed it in dog poop. I started to vomit and crawled out of the cellar without seeing and or counting the pups. I could not stop vomiting. My boss called Ian and they took me to the doctor and that was when I found out I was PREGNANT!

Unearthing the Diamond

Our Son, Ayale

How could I possibly be pregnant? I was almost at the end of my period! I was confused but also overjoyed as finally I would have someone for myself!

Ian, who doesn't usually show any emotions, was elated. He knew how much this meant to me and I knew that as a Rastaman, he would never marry me but I felt sure he would stay with me forever. I could not stop vomiting or being sick. I disliked the smell of anything and even water tasted bitter. I lost so much weight I was sure there was no way I could keep the baby.

January 1979 came and by the end of the month, I started to have another period. Ian took me to the hospital where I was hospitalized and an IV drip inserted into my arm. Immediately the vomiting would stop but if the drip came out, the vomiting would restart. The nurse tried inserting the IV into my arm for the second time but could not find my veins since they had collapsed. Using the needle to slash open the skin, she exposed vein; reinserting the drip. I was in so much pain and today, I still bear that scar.

I was in hospital for a few days and one night I started having contractions. I was two months pregnant and as the bleeding got worse, I started passing large clots. I felt afraid and began crying. The nurse on duty was so sorry for me when she explained that I had lost the baby and would need a Dilatation and Curettage the following morning.

I was told by the nurse to go downstairs and be examined by the doctor who would schedule the D&C for later that day. As I headed downstairs, I met Ian on the way up to see me (he would visit first thing every morning) and right there on the stairs I told him I had lost the baby, his only response was to ask if the doctor had examined me. I told him no.

When we reached the doctor's office, she explained to us that the amount of blood and clotting I had experienced indicated I had lost the baby and she was going to do a D&C. She advised us to wait for six months before trying to conceive again. Ian asked if she had examined me. She said there was no need to since the nurse and my chart indicated the huge amount of blood I had passed there was no way a baby could still be inside me.

Ian told her he would *not* sign the consent form until she had examined me as he was positive I was still pregnant. She complied and the moment she examined between my legs, she started saying this isn't possible. Ian asked, "What's wrong?" She replied, "The cervix is closed she is still pregnant!" I could not believe my ears. *I had passed so much blood, how could I still be pregnant?* She sent for a wheelchair and had me wheeled back to the ward where I would remain on bed rest but before we left her office she remarked to Ian, "Whatever God you pray to, don't stop, there is no explanation for her to still be pregnant." I stayed in the hospital for about two more weeks then I was released and sent home.

In my fourth month I began enjoying being pregnant. The vomiting stopped and I was able to eat whatever I wanted. I remember dancing for Ian with the belly as we watched my body change from being slender to round. I seemed to grow daily. Actually, I didn't really want a daughter, not for my first baby. I wanted a son to carry on Ian's name. He wanted a son too.

On Sunday, July 22, 1979 we went swimming at Blue Lagoon. I loved to go swimming with Ian; he taught me how to swim and would usually make me hold onto his shoulders as we swam especially if I became tired. We swam across the Blue lagoon from edge to edge, I was wearing a yellow leotard and when we got out of the water people were surprised we had swum across and back with the belly, I was seven months and two weeks. That night as we lay in bed, Ian was stroking my belly as the baby kicked. He often spoke to the baby while he stroked my belly. That night he said, "If you are a boy kick once, if you are a girl kick twice." I laughed and asked why the girl got the hardest task but before I could finish the question, sure enough the baby kicked once again and settled down. Ian was now convinced we were having a boy.

The next morning was Monday, July 23, 1979. We got out of bed and I made breakfast. We went to the living room, sat on the couch eating and looking at the view. Suddenly I had the urge to stand and so I did. The second I stood up I felt the water rushing down my legs. Ian asked if I had peed on myself. I said I didn't know, I just felt like standing up and water just began flowing. It would not stop so we went to the courtyard and it was there I realized it was not water, this was so slimy and I said to Ian that my water must've broke. He rushed for a shower curtain for me to stand on and later told me to take a shower while he went to get a taxi. I needed to get to the hospital. When he got back I was laughing. I was having contractions but they were bearable. I asked if this is the pain women said was unbearable.

The taxi arrived and I was taken to the hospital. On the way, the pain began to get stronger but I was still able to bear it. When we got to the hospital we registered and I was sent to the maternity ward. We walked to the maternity ward and Ian told the nurse his wife was in labour and the water had busted. She asked him where I was, I was standing right there but I was seven months pregnant and even though I thought my belly was big it appeared small compared to all the other women on the ward who were all full term. Ian smiled and told her I was right there.

I was given a bed and told the doctor would see me when he did his rounds. The nurse was uncertain whether the doctor would try to make the pregnancy go longer since I was only seven months and two weeks pregnant. When the doctor came, he said I was dilated and he would have to deliver the baby within twenty four hours, but could not guarantee the baby's health, or even if the baby would make it. Ian had to go home and leave me alone at the hospital and that night I was introduced to the level of pain a mother feels when she is truly in labour. Since I wore dreadlocks, I was fearful and didn't want to cry out as I heard the stories about nurses beating women who created a scene during labour; so I bit my lips so as not to cry out aloud.

The next morning, Tuesday, July 24, 1979, Ian came, bringing me breakfast and a change of clothes. I tried hiding the amount of pain I was in, from him and trying to be strong, I turned my head away whenever the pain came and the tears ran down my

Unearthing the Diamond

face. You could count the number of teeth in my head from the imprint they left on my lips. I cried silently.

I remember an older woman who was giving birth to her eighth child. She was in so much pain but not contractions. Her teeth were all rotten in the front and she kept crying about her teeth. 'Whoa, Whoa! Me teeth! Lord have mercy! Me would gi anyting fi feel de belly pain, eight pickney and a don't know wha baby pain feel like, all me feel a teeth ache. Whoa me teeth.' In my own pain I thought that was funny and being as young as I was, I laughed through my contractions. There was another woman who chose to lay on her belly. I still cannot understand how she was able to.

I was in labour from Monday morning at about 8 when the water broke until midnight, Tuesday. *How much longer was this going to take?* I felt the urge to use the toilet and so hobbled to the bathroom, holding onto the rails of each bed as I made my way. When I got there I would sit on the toilet and tried, straining but to no avail.

Tamika Felina Pommells Williams

Suddenly a nurse called out. "Who is that?"

I said, "Me."

"Me who?" asked the nurse.

"Tamika." I said.

"Go back to your bed and use the bedpan, you can have de baby in de toilet you know."

"No," I said. "I want to dodo."

The nurse was a nice woman who liked me and said, "Come to the delivery and room let me check you out."

So I hobbled to the delivery room and she helped me onto the bed, positioning me, then she said, "The baby is crowning."

"Crowning?" I asked.

She said, "I can see the head."

The baby was coming and suddenly I forgot about the pain. *The baby was coming!* When Ian came he would see the baby and at exactly 4:20 a.m. on Wednesday, July 25th 1979 my son was born. I was the happiest woman alive.

Unearthing the Diamond

He was so tiny, weighing 3¾ pounds and was immediately placed in an incubator to help him breathe. His forehead was also not fully developed and ridges were visible. The nurse said this was normal in premature babies because they weren't completely developed. During the delivery she cut me twice in order for his head to come out and the following morning I had to go the operating theatre to be stitched up. I spent the rest of the time in the delivery room so I could be near to the baby.

Me a mom. Even though he was tiny, I didn't care.

When Ian finally came I gave him the news: *WE HAD A SON!* And suddenly it dawned on me that we didn't even have a name for him. Ian returned that evening and told me his name was Mikael Ayale and I told him I preferred Ayale Mikael.

When the doctor examined him he said he was jaundiced. I didn't even know what that meant but the doctor said it wasn't serious and all I needed to do was to hold him in direct sunlight and it would go away. It took about a week for it to go away and during this time my son lost some of his birth weight

- he was down to one and a half pound. He was now smaller than when he was born. But for me, I didn't care he had ten fingers and toes. I knew I had enough love to give him and he would grow. After two weeks we were both released from the hospital and I got to take my son home.

Having and taking care of a baby was surreal. He was so tiny yet perfectly made. He looked like a white baby and his hair was so straight. He loved me. The most special part of being a mom for me was breast feeding.

Ian was the PERFECT dad. He made sure I was comfortable and helped with the baby. One day in particular, I remember Ayale was crying non-stop. I didn't know what to do so I picked him up and he immediately stopped crying. After a few minutes, I put him back in his crib and sure enough the crying started again. Ian was adamant that I should *not* pick him up. He said I was going to spoil him.

I argued that he was just a baby and didn't know any different. Ian said, 'If you can't bear to hear him crying, just go for a walk. When you get back he would've stopped crying."

I didn't want a fight with Ian so I went for a walk.

All the way while I was walking, I could still hear him crying and after walking for about five minutes I decided to turn around. I told myself I didn't care if Ian was going to be upset, I was picking up *my* baby. But when I opened the door, to my surprise, Ayale was sound asleep - but in a temper.

You could hear him breathing but Ian insisted that once he was fed, dried and learnt how to play by himself without growing dependent on being held, he would be independent. Ian said if I didn't start now, when he got older it would be sleepless nights for me.

Of course Ian was right. Ayale began looking around when he wasn't asleep and was what most would call a good baby. I could feed him, burp him, play with him a bit then put him in his crib or on my bed and he would play with his hanging mobile or coo to the birds out the window and sleep when he wanted.

He grew fast and was no longer a tiny baby.

I have never seen such a tiny baby grow so fast. When he turned four months old, he was the same size of a full term baby at four months but there was one major problem; he refused to drink baby formula. All he wanted was the breast and water. He would *not* even take juice, this meant I had to be with him all the time but I didn't care. He was mine.

Shortly before he turned six months old I noticed his navel remained distended. Before, when he was relaxed it would go back in but this time it stayed out. I took him to Dr. Vashanti (a Cuban doctor working at Port Antonio Hospital) and she said there was nothing to worry about. She said that I was a young mother and that I was overreacting and even laughed; so we took him back home.

The next day when it was time for his morning bath as I was bathing him, I passed the washcloth over his tummy and the wail that came out of his little mouth had Ian running to see. I was just as surprised as Ian when I explained what happened. Ayale would not stop crying and this was indeed a cry of pain. We took him out of the water and dried him as best we could since we could not touch his tummy. His navel seemed bigger than before and red.

We returned to the hospital and when he was re-examined we were told we needed to take him to the Bustamante Hospital for Children in Kingston. We were dirt poor and didn't even have the fare to go to Kingston but Ian went to Frenchman's Cove hotel and borrowed some money from the manager, Mr. Frank Lawrence. We headed to Kingston that night, taking him straight to the hospital with the letter of referral from the Pt. Antonio Hospital.

This was when I met Dr William Dennis (Bill). He told us Ayale had a condition called a strangulated hernia. I looked at him, my eyes and mouth wide opened. A strangulated what? Dr. Dennis explained that somehow some of his intestine got into his navel and the opening closed locking the intestine in and this was the problem, it could be corrected but would need surgery straight away.

I started to cry and ask God: *Why, why was this happening to my baby?* I struggled to keep him inside me and now this. Ian, as usual, was the strong one.

He said we were blessed and lucky to have taken him in before it got any worse and since the surgery could correct it, he would be ok.

In a way, Ian had two children - Ayale and me.

Dr Dennis and his team performed the surgery on Ayale that same night and we stayed at the hospital till it was over and taken to recovery. Dr Dennis told us to go home and return the next day because he would be sleeping all night. Ian's mom was living in Kingston and so we stayed with her. That night I didn't sleep and cried like a baby. This was the first time I wasn't with my baby since he was born; even when he had jaundice, I remained with him in hospital. This time I felt as if I was going to die.

The next morning we were at the hospital before visiting hours. The nurses somehow understood my need to be with my baby and I was allowed in. They were breaking the rules and allowing me to see him before the doctors came on the wards. I was so thankful.

Ayale was awake but looked so weak and sad. His tummy looked completely covered with a bandage. I picked him up carefully and breast-fed him. He suckled as the nurses came and told me to go outside before the doctors came. I did. Before the doctors left, I spotted Dr Dennis. He saw me and walking over to us he told us that the surgery went well. We could take Ayala home within a week - A WEEK! That seemed like forever but I was so happy he was going to be ok.

By the end of the week we took him home and every time I saw or touched his tummy, my stomach turned as there was now a scar where his navel used to be.

Thankfully, he recovered so quickly from the surgery and started to regain weight.

I felt truly blessed to have him and every day I would hold him, listen to him coo or cry, touch, breastfeed and love him; he was so precious. I was complete! I loved this baby more than life itself.

Ayale brought so much joy into our lives! Ian would often look at us and laugh. Though he hardly ever said he loved me, I could see the adoration in his eyes whenever he looked at us.

Two months after the surgery, when Ayale was eight months old, I noticed he began losing weight but it seemed his tummy was growing. One morning I picked him up and heard water sloshing around in his belly. He was looking pale and would not breastfeed so we returned to the hospital, where we saw the same doctor, Dr. Vashanti.

I vividly recall him being surrounded by doctors as I stood and watched the nurse sticking my baby eighteen times trying to find a vein for an IV. Eighteen times. I was so weak from crying. Every time he was stuck I felt his pain. I felt so helpless when I heard his wails, standing by and unable to do anything. Finally, they decided he had to be sent to the Bustamante Children's Hospital in Kingston. Here we go again. This time he was referred to see Dr. Barbara Johnson.

When we got to her office, she sent us to The Bustamante's Hospital surgical ward. She said he has a condition called Ascites which meant his liver was malfunctioning and there was fluid on his stomach. He also had an enlarged testicle and she wanted the surgeon to do a biopsy to see if the two conditions were related. This was March 1980 and this would be the longest, most trying time in my life as a young mother.

Dr Dennis was again Ayale's surgeon. It was only two months ago he had operated on our baby and here we were again, It seemed Dr. Dennis saw my concern because he spoke with Ian and me and reassured us that all he was going to do was take a sample to send to the lab to be tested and this surgery would take half an hour tops.

The morning of the operation for the biopsy, Ian and I were early. As usual, something deep within made me so scared and even though the doctor was reassuring, I could not help myself. I was a nervous wreck and could not stop crying. Ian as always was the positive one who tried to calm me but I was inconsolable.

We waited in the waiting area of the operating theater.

Half an hour came and went, then one hour then two hours. *What was happening? Why was it taking so long?* Dr Dennis said less than half an hour, now it was more than two hours. Dr Johnson came out of surgery and I tried to ask her what was happening but she said we had to wait till the surgeon came out to speak with us.

Exactly two and a half hours later after our baby was wheeled into surgery Dr. Dennis finally came out. There was a small jar in his hand. He said the surgery had taken longer than he thought because of what he saw when he went in and held up the jar. It looked like a small kidney. He said when he opened the sack to do the biopsy on the right testicle; it was covered in what looked like sores which he pointed out to us.

My mind was going crazy, *what was he talking about?* Then he said it looked like a malignant tumor. Then he said it - *it was cancerous*. I stared at him blankly. Continuing, he said he had seen it so many times and so decided to remove it. I was numb. *What was I hearing?* Then he said the most heartless thing I had ever heard. He gave us the jar with some papers and told us to take it to Nutthall lab, straight

Unearthing the Diamond

away, so that he could have the confirmation immediately. Ian was speechless!

We both walked the two or so miles to the lab with Ian carrying a piece of our son in his hand. We left the testicle at the lab and returned to the hospital to be there when Ayale woke up. We were allowed to see him in the recovery room where he was sleeping so soundly. We left and returned to Ian's mom's home. I couldn't be consoled. *Why, good God, why was this happening to me? Why was my baby fighting for his life? Why did God give me this baby to then take him away so soon? How could he be suffering so much since he was only eight months old?* I prayed to God to spare his life and take mine instead. I cried and cried and cried.

The next morning we were back at the hospital and they had received the report from the lab. It was official. It was confirmed. Ayale had a malignant tumor and now they needed to do other tests to see if it was connected to the Ascites. It was. The doctors gave him two months to live. I wanted to die. *How much could I endure?*

I began looking back on all the sad and bad experiences in my life, *was God punishing me? When will I just be happy? When would things just go right for me?* But one thing after the other was happening and I couldn't cope. I needed my mother. I needed my baby. Good God, I need You.

The Big "C"

Finally it sunk in, our son was diagnosed with cancer and according to the doctor, throughout known medical history, only four other babies had it - and they all had died. I was completely devastated! I cried so much my eyes seemed permanently swollen.

Ian had to return to Portland where we lived, leaving me at his mom's in Kingston, where I could visit Ayale every day. At just eight months, I was his food supply and so I had to be at the hospital, to feed and express milk for him.

It was a scary time and for the first time, I was on my own -- without Ian. Everyday when visiting Ayale, I would ride the Number 27 bus up Mountain View Avenue, passing my old high school. It left me feeling empty. For the first time since being with Ian, I was lost, and, like a robot, doing normal everyday things but knowing within me, I was dying.

So many questions.

The one that stuck in my mind was WHY? I was still a child, only 18 years old and here I was, struggling, trying to make sense of what was happening to my son, me and Ian. We had no money and staying with Ian's mom, who had her family to take care off. I felt like I was an added burden. I saw, and could sense, the stress my being in her home caused.

Every morning I drank a cup of cornmeal porridge then head off to the hospital. There I would spend all my days before leaving at 5p.m. to return to my mother-in-law. This was a daily routine.

At the hospital, Ayale seemed to be in so much pain. His tummy grew and was so distended that the shirts he wore were unable to button. He was so uncomfortable that his head was constantly pushed back. I spent many days just trying to make him as comfortable as possible and to let him know I was there and loved him. This went on for four months.

I remember one morning a nurse told me to stay away. "He is hanging on because you keep coming," she said. I told myself that morning 'if that was the case I would stay longer' and that was what I started doing. I began leaving the hospital at seven p.m. instead. However, no one could explain why he was still alive. His crib was pushed into a corner as we waited on him to die and my heart ached to see him the way he was. Still I was thankful he was alive. All this time, Ian was alone in Portland; fasting, praying, putting ashes on his head and worrying about his dying son and his helpless woman, a mere child herself.

One morning I lost all self control! I made a big fuss with Ian's mom. I told her she was unfeeling, uncaring and a terrible grandmother. I accused her of not caring for her grandson and begged her to come to see him in the hospital. I guess she was under her own stresses (with a sick husband to care for) but I was near breaking point, unable to hold up on my own anymore. I needed support. Eventually, we cried together and finally she decided to visit Ayale with me that morning.

I hated to see Ayale suffering. Somehow, I felt, from the day before, he was not going to make it. He looked so pale and hardly responding to anything. I was sure he would be dead when I walked in and didn't want to be alone to face this. Thanks to God for small mercies! That morning my mother-in-law came with me.

When we got to the hospital I looked gingerly into the ward. He was in his crib, completely covered with transparent plastic. The night before, he had slipped into a coma and was unable to breath. He was being given oxygen. I looked at him and he looked so rubbery. His little feet were now BLUE! I rushed out and called Dr. Johnson who was on the ward. I was hysterical but she was so calm. Her response to my asking why his gums and feet were blue was: *"There's nothing to be done for him now. He's dying."* Then she added, *"When someone is dying the circulation leaves the feet first. He's dying."*

I just stared at her a blank stare on my face while Mama hugged me and said, "Tammy, this is no time for crying, it's time for prayer."

Dr. Johnson looked at her and said, "Prayer can't help him now, he's too far gone." Mama got so upset at her! She looked at the doctor and said, "My God can do anything!"

I don't even recall how I returned to his crib. Mama was saying I should call Ian. Ian needed to be here before he died. I felt a pit in my stomach, an emptiness I had never experienced before. I felt helplessness, confusion, frustration and finally resignation and told myself he had suffered enough. I promised I would never forget him and that I would always love him. I closed my eyes knowing he was leaving me forever.

I called Frenchman's Cove Hotel leaving a message with the manager, Mr. Frank Lawrence, asking him to get word to Ian to come to Kingston immediately as his baby was dying. There were no cellphones and only the hotels and a few business places had landline phones.

Back in Kingston, Ian's mom insisted I should leave the hospital and return home to wait for Ian. There was only one bus out of Portland and it would not be in Kingston before 10 p.m. I was certain Ian wouldn't get to see him alive. But I couldn't sleep or cry anymore. I started worrying about where we were going to get the money from to bury Ayale.

At almost 10:30, Ian knocked on the door. He said he wanted to go straight to the hospital but I told him they wouldn't let us in since visiting time was over. He insisted. We walked to the road and stopped by a home owned by a Rastaman called Peter Ray. He had a car and did not hesitate when we told him our dilemma. Without a question, he drove us directly to the hospital.

When we got there, the nurse was about to tell us we couldn't enter but she saw the look on Ian's face. She must've known that he had every intention to see his son, come what may, and so she let the three of us in. Ian just stood there looking at Ayale, never saying a word. His mouth was moving but nothing came out. I don't know why, but I felt scared and didn't know how to cope with everything. I didn't know how to comfort Ian. I looked down at our baby and saw Ian's tears falling on his exposed belly. This was the first time I had ever seen Ian cry and they were magical since in that instant Ayale opened his eyes and looked at his dad. He then slipped away again.

Ian put his hand around me and pulled me to his side and said: *"It will be ok, Tamika it will be ok"*.

We drove back to his mom's house in silence. Something had happened in the hospital and none of us wanted to speak or question what it was. For me, I grasped at any hint of hope.

"It'll be ok!" Ian had promised.

Tamika Felina Pommells Williams

He's Awake

The next morning I was anxious to get to the hospital. Ian wanted to wait till the doctor's ran ward but I just wanted to get over with it. Ian said, "Tamika, trust me, if he died they would have called." That seemed to make sense but I needed to find out for myself.

Finally we got to the hospital and I searched the ward for Ayala's crib. My heart skipped a beat as I didn't see the plastic over his crib. I squeezed Ian's hand as we walked over to his crib. He was there; awake; though his eyes looked clearer, he did seem a little sick.

The next few weeks I had renewed hope in my heart. The doctors had given him less than twenty-four hours to live and that had passed! Soon days passed into weeks and he was getting stronger. He was still alive!

During this time something strange began to happen to Ayale.

Unearthing the Diamond

After he woke from the coma, bumps came out over his body, from the crown of his head to the soles of his tiny feet and within a short time he was completely covered. The bumps grew and oozed pus. And every morning as I entered the ward I knew he was alive because of the stench. It was as if he was rotting away. Soon the bumps turned into sores and the more they came out, the more his swollen tummy shrunk. Dr Dennis remarked that it seemed the cancer was somehow turning to the outside of his body. I guess he saw the hope in my eyes and warned me that any day I could come and find that he had died.

I remember meeting a Rasta lady whose name I have now forgotten. She had a son named Ababe. He was on the surgical ward as Ayale and we would speak daily. Her son had a hole in his heart. One day she asked me the meaning of Ayale's name and I told her I didn't know because his dad was the one who gave him the name Mikeal Ayale. I just switched them around.

She said she believed a child's name is very important and promised to look in an African book she had for the meaning. The following day she brought a book filled with names and I saw the name Ayale. There was just one single word. LIFE!

My hope and faith hung onto the meaning of his name.

He was alive and had a life to live! I hoped he would make it to his first birthday which was less than a month away. She also brought another book to share with me titled *Back to Eden* by Jethro Kloss. It was a herbal book and it spoke about how he treated cancer patients giving them carrot juice. I made a mental note, if I ever had the chance I would ply my son with carrot juice. A few days later when I was visiting Ayale I was told that Ababe passed away during the night. I never saw his mom again.

My son looked so much like a leper. The sores and smell sometimes unbearable to me as his mom but I cuddled him, loving and praying he would make a complete recovery.

Unearthing the Diamond

The sores became open and raw but he seemed more comfortable. His tummy was now down to a normal size and eventually, the sores were healing. He was now in the hospital for four whole months laying on his back and I needed to get him home. I asked the doctors if I could take him home for his first birthday. This was July 20th, 1980 and in five days July 25th, it would be a year.

I could not believe my ears when Dr Dennis said he would allow me to take him home for a week. *Was I hearing correctly? I could take my baby home?* I got word to Ian, "We're coming home."

A nurse said to me the day we were leaving the hospital, "Take lots of pictures because he won't see another birthday."

When we arrived in Portland the first thing I bought was several pounds of carrot. Ian looked at me as if I were mad. Here we were with our sick son and I didn't get cereal, I got carrots. Whenever Ayale was hungry he would get carrot juice mixed with milk. When he was thirsty, I gratered carrot and he drank that for water. Every thing he had for the week, was homemade and of carrot.

July 25th 1980 came and we NEVER took a photograph of him since we both decided he would be remembered without photographs and forever kept alive in our hearts. Ian insisted he would be around for many more birthdays and I hung onto his every word. A week after we got him home, we had to return to the hospital. Dr Dennis could NOT believe this was the same baby, when he saw him. He said colour had returned to his cheeks and he seemed to have finally gained some weight.

"What have you done with him?" He asked.

Ian laughed and said, "Doc, all she feeds him with is carrots. Carrot morning, evening, noon and night."

Dr Dennis laughed. Ian told him he was serious.

Dr Dennis added that carrots helped to clean the system and helped to rid the body of waste. That was all I needed to hear. If they allowed me to take him home again, by God I would NOT stop feeding him carrots!

Unearthing the Diamond

Suddenly Dr. Dennis said the unthinkable, "Since he has done so well at home for this week I am releasing him to you for another two weeks but make sure he gets more than carrots."

I was overjoyed. I asked if he was being released from hospital. Dr Dennis said no, he wasn't. I needed to return with him in two weeks and then we would know how well he was doing.

On returning home, I made him porridge, soup, juice and added carrots to everything. When he drank a bottle of water it was water made from carrots - plain, unsweetened carrot juice.

For six months, we had to return to the hospital every two weeks and everybody marveled at his recovery. On the sixth month visit, Dr. Dennis told us there was no way he could've been diagnosed correctly since there was no explanation for him being alive. He actually said that they must've misdiagnosed him.

I did not allow that to dampen my spirits and asked if that meant he never had cancer. He said, "Yes he did," The way he had recovered pointed to a type of cancer that went into remission and could reappear at any time, maybe in a few months, a few years but he wouldn't make it through his childhood years.

Ian saw the dread in my eyes and it was as if he could read my mind, "Tamika," he said, as we walked with Ayale, "they are doctors, they believe in medicine. It's easier to say they're wrong than to admit a miracle has happened. Our son is *cured*!"

This visit to the hospital was special because now he was discharged from the hospital and was given an appointment to visit the hospital's clinic in six months. Ayale wasted no time. It was as if he wanted to make up for lost time. He ate everything! He played and when he laughed it made my belly turn, it was so sweet and special. He was slow in most areas for an eighteen month old child but we told ourselves that was because he was laying on his back for four months when he would've been exploring the world.

One day, a door slammed and I realized that he wasn't hearing properly. We were in the bedroom and he didn't turn his head toward the sound. I panicked and called Ian, who came running. "What happen Tamika?" He asked.

"The baby can't hear." I said while Ayale, looking at his father, grinned from ear-to-ear.

"Then how does he know I'm here?"

I decided to take notice of everything so I could tell Dr Dennis on our next visit.

On our next visit Dr. Dennis confirmed my fears; Ayale was deaf in both ears. He referred us to a Dr Charles Lyn, an ENT Specialist, who recommended he be fitted with hearing aids. Dr. Dennis said that the deafness could've been the side effect of the anti-cancer drug he had been given. But I didn't care that he was deaf, all I cared about was he was alive, healthy and loved by me.

We couldn't afford the cost of a hearing aid as the 80's was a difficult time for Jamaica. As a teenage mother with a sick baby, it seemed my life was hard. I recalled being without money at one point and worse yet NOTHING was in the shops. The shelves were always empty with no milk, sugar, washing soap nor even bathing soap. I remembered at one time after Ayale was home from the hospital I wanted to make him some porridge. We had no milk or sugar and all we were able to get at the shop was a bottle of strawberry syrup. The owner of the shop was related to Ian's family and that was the only reason we were able to buy it. Everything was *'married'* to something else (in other words, if we wanted the bottle of syrup, we had to purchase something we couldn't afford or didn't even want).

We took the syrup home, boiled the cornmeal and sweetened it with the syrup. It was the first time in my life I had seen porridge sweetened with syrup and it was pink.

Ayale didn't mind. It was sweet and he loved porridge. It became a ritual making porridge for him everyday which he had during the days especially when there was nothing else to eat. Sometimes all we were able to afford was something for Ayale to eat and we often went without. Life had its challenges living in Portland, but we found time to play and be thankful for the little we had.

Unearthing the Diamond

Ayale was a beautiful baby who looked like both Ian and I; his hair blond, fuzzy and natty. He hated having it combed and so I often braided it and it would be weeks later before it was redone. He would suck his right thumb and caress the ear of his favourite stuffed toy - a yellow elephant. It was a complicated task of sucking his thumb since in the same hand was the elephant, and the index finger caressing the tip of his nose.

Ayale is my entire life. We couldn't afford hearing aids and as a result, he was unable to speak up to the age of seven years of age. His vocabulary consisted of two words: "Mama and Papa". He used his eyes and hands to point or some other gesticulation. He decided he'd communicate by drawing; that was how we communicated daily. He quickly developed his own way of communicating through art and when he was almost eight-years-old we were able to purchase his first hearing aids. He slowly began to speak. His first sentence came after seeing his friend Omar being hit by a car during lunch break at school.

Tamika Felina Pommells Williams

Ayale today, is in his 30s. A graduate of Herbert Morrison Comprehensive High School and a qualified graphic artist with a Diploma from the Art Institute of Fort Lauderdale, he is a businessman with equal shares in our family business, Ahhh...Ras Natango Gallery & Garden.

Yes he wears hearing aids even today but he lives his life knowing he has so much to contribute and he is the first to state he is not handicapped. Life owes him no favours. He is my son in whom I am well pleased.

Survival

Living in Portland had many challenges. There was no future for us as we did everything necessary to survive but we were dirt poor raising a baby.

Ian did every possible thing trying to provide for us. I taught him to make straw mats and he would walk from door-to-door for miles each day trying to sell them. He often came home with a defeated look on his face and I knew he sold none. Once in a while one would be sold and he would return home with a plastic bag full of food he had bought. We would celebrate by cooking up a feast, make love and imagine better days.

I knitted sweaters, tams and booties for babies which Ian would sell in the market, sometimes for less than the cost of the yarn. We would ask friends to bring yarn from the USA and so we were able to sell the baby's sets at the cost of the yarn with nothing for the skill or time in making them. To have a variety of things to sell at the market Ian bought leather sandals and resold out of the back of our old car along with the things I knitted.

Tamika Felina Pommells Williams

The car had a name. It was called "TERROR", a 1971 Cortina. It was white and needed a lot of body work. Its floor was so old; we had to be careful when we placed our feet on it. When driving in it, the exhaust fumes would almost suffocate us. I usually had to hang my head out from the window just to breathe.

The struggle to feed ourselves became so daunting and Ian, who was my Saviour, became verbally abusive. I could see and feel his frustrations which would make me frustrated too. I began to feel sorry for myself and wished that my life could be different. I wished for a normal childhood but instead here I was a teenager, being a housewife and mother and shouldering the responsibilities of a woman when I needed mothering myself.

Whenever Ian lost it and said things he regretted, he would get so quiet and meditate which made me feel so inadequate. Later he would counsel me and apologize for things he had said. He never gave up and promised me things WOULD get better if we stuck together.

Unearthing the Diamond

It seemed to me that everyone was expecting us to fail since there was no external support from either of our families. Ian's mom loved him and thought I was too much of a burden on him. It was just Ian, Ayale and I; it seemed, against the entire world.

In a bid to survive we tried everything in Portland. We started a dance troupe at Titchfield High School and helped motivate young people to take pride in themselves. It wasn't profitable financially but we had fun and I loved dancing on stage with the Acid dance group (three men).

I recalled how I used to just sleep away my days. I would sleep while Ian went in search of food, leaving me home with Ayale, hungry, without even a radio or television. I slept to pass the time until he came home with something, anything to eat. Once, I complained about sleeping my life away since I slept so much till I was tired (if that was possible).

Ian's wise retort was, "Take the rest and sleep now while you can, there'll come a time when you'll be so busy and you'd wish for these days of nothing to do."

I was upset at his response because I couldn't see the future and all I kept hearing were promises. Empty promises, I said to myself. I saw no way out of Portland, out of our poverty and here he was telling me about better days when I would be so busy and no time for sleep.

I can say, we experienced every test a married couple could have and through it all I couldn't understand how one could remain as positive as Ian was. With every blow he got, he took it with a smile and with the dawn of a new day move forward confidently stating, "My God will not let me sit on the sidewalks to beg bread."

I began to rely on his words and opinions more than I did the Bible and finally, one day he told me, "Tamika, I'm not God. You need to find Him for yourself."

I believed in God but I didn't have the kind of faith Ian had. I told him I didn't know where to start and he gave me a Bible and told me to start at the beginning - Genesis 1. That began my personal walk with God as I began reading a chapter a day.

Unearthing the Diamond

Sometimes I read for entertainment as there was nothing else to do but I got to know all the stories, skipping over the parts about who beget whom.

Ian eventually concluded that Portland was NOT the place for us. He likened the parish to a woman of the night. A whore. Every idea we had and tried did not bear fruit and so, he finally reiterated that Portland was a stagnant parish with no future for anyone. The mentality of the residents coupled with the lack of opportunities was enough to break anyone. Ian said that Portland enticed us with its beauty, gave us hope and then dashed them away. Whatever little money we invested in our ideas, just vanished. A whore he said. Portland was a whore.

The poverty and suffering in Portland wore us out and dashed our many dreams, like the water in the ocean. From infidelity to lack of food, to lack of emotional support and eventually discovering that the parish held no future; Ian decided we needed to move to greener pastures. So we gave away all our furniture and belongings, packed what little clothes we had in an orange suitcase and said our goodbyes to Portland. Taking a country bus to Kingston, we spent the night in Harbor View at Ian's mom, then the following day, boarded a train for Montego Bay.

Before settling on moving to Montego Bay, Ian had scouted out Ocho Rios as well. He often went to Ocho Rios which was at least two hours away from where we lived in Portland and he would take the items he painted and carved, along with the things I knitted, to the cruise ship pier to sell to the tourists. This meant running from the police as it was against the law to sell to tourists at the pier, in those days.

Montego Bay was a larger city and we decided if we lived in Montego Bay it would be easier for us to survive as there was sure to be better opportunities for making money than in Portland. We had no family or friends in Mo-Bay (its well-known name) but we had been together without family and believed as long as we had each other we could face ANYTHING! I was excited, as well as scared. Portland was our home and with all its difficulties and hardship at least I knew my way around. *Where would Ayale go to school? Where would we live?*

Unearthing the Diamond

Would things really get better with us moving away from this parish Ian called a whore?

That night, Ian's mom prayed for us and we ate the dinner she cooked and as we discussed the adventure we were about to embark on, come the dawn. I couldn't sleep that night.

Tamika Felina Pommells Williams

Montego Bay, Here We Come!

Sitting in the train, taking us cross country from one end of the island to the other. We had looked at the train before as it passed and imagined travelling on it and now, here we were. There were so many dreams, so many possibilities. A bright future lay ahead.

This was my very first train ride.

It was amazing. The little wooden houses along the rails were fascinating. Finally the train stopped. We had reached our destination.

We arrived in Montego Bay the 31st December, 1986. We got off the train and suddenly, it dawned on me, we had nowhere to spend the night, nowhere to go. Both Ayale and I looked at Ian trusting him and his decision to take us to this strange place. Looking around the railway station, I was unafraid since our small family was together. Our future depended on this move and Ian looked confident. He was a man with a mission. After living in Portland for nine years, moving to Montego Bay had to hold better prospects

Unearthing the Diamond

for us as it could not be worse than Portland, financially.

We walked outside the railway station and Ian hailed a taxi. He told the driver to take us to the nearest guest house. The driver told us there was one at the top of the road and he would gladly take us there. We boarded the taxi and headed up Railway Lane, in less than two minutes we stopped at the top of Railway Lane and Barnett Street. I looked outside and saw the sign, Lloyd's Intensified Inn.

We walked into the inn and inquired about the cost. It was $60 Jamaican per night and we smiled to ourselves. There were rooms upstairs, a restaurant downstairs and even a club on the upper floor. The room was small but clean, it had a small bathroom and we put our single suitcase into a small closet and settled in. After eating dinner that evening in the restaurant, we put Ayale to bed and decided to have a drink at the club later that night.

As we entered the club it became clear. This was a whore house! The club was no ordinary club. On a makeshift stage in front of us was a young woman no older than 18 years old, she was naked and there was a lit cigarette in her vagina puffing away. I had NEVER seen anything like this before in my life. My mouth must have dropped to the floor and Ian gently squeezed my hand as he led me back to our room. There was no need for discussion, we had to find a proper place to live and we decided to move the next day. This was no place to live with our seven-year old son.

The following day we headed to a community named Granville where we were able to rent two furnished rooms opposite the Granville All Age School. We registered Ayale at the school and felt a renewed sense of hope. We would survive in this city.

Ayale was perfect in every way when you looked at him.

He was the most beautiful boy I had ever seen, except when he opened his mouth as he was unable to speak. At the age of seven he could only say two words clearly - Mama and Dadda. He would also point his finger in a direction to help him to communicate. I used to be so embarrassed when he tried to speak as people would stare. He also communicated by drawing. If he wanted a ripe banana he would draw and colour a banana.

One day his new teacher, Mrs. Lawrence saw me tugging at his arm trying to shut him up. She called me aside. She said, "Mrs. Williams, nothing is wrong with Ayale. He cannot speak to express himself because he doesn't have hearing aids but he must express himself. When he comes to school he's in my care. Please don't embarrass him by trying to prevent him from communicating just because you are embarrassed."

I was ashamed but when I walked away I was comforted that she was his teacher; she cared enough about him as her student, enough to scold me his mother.

During our first few months living in Montego Bay we were able to purchase one hearing aid for Ayale. It was his first hearing aid.

His doctor told us that now he was able to hear the words being said more clearly that we should get him a second hearing aid as soon as we could afford it because he would hear better with both. Hearing better meant he would soon be speaking. This was after checking beneath his tongue, which stretched way past his bottom lip. The doctor suggested another reason for a child having difficulties speaking was a cleft palate (the tongue is unable to move and stretch past the lower lip. Having had Ayale do the exercise of sticking out his tongue and it stretched past his lower lip the doctor informed us that he was confident Ayale would eventually speak if he had two hearing aids.

I remember Dr. Dennis telling us to not act shocked or surprised when he finally spoke. He added that Ayale was now hearing what was being said and would speak any time soon, but we shouldn't make an event of it as we might cause him further damage if we make him aware he was "different." In short I was to stay calm.

Ayale would always come home for lunch. I would've prepared enough for him to share with any of his friends who came home with him. This specific day he rushed home. I was standing at the wash tub washing when he came running to me.

"Mummy, Mummy!" He shouted.

"Car hit down Omar!"

I looked at him in shock. "What did you say?" I asked.

He looked calmly at me and said, "Car lick down Omar!"

I was delirious. My son's first sentence! I screamed for Ian. "Ian! Ian! Come quick! Ayale talking! Him Bumboclatt talking!"

I picked him up, swinging him around. He looked at me with a question in his eyes as if to say: *why are you so excited? I've always spoken?*

Ian, being the voice of reason, came out calmly and said, "Tell me, son what happened to Omar."

I had completely forgotten about his friend and now, he pulled his Dad's hand, taking him to the scene of Omar's accident. I know the emphasis should have been on Omar being hit by a car but hearing my son, over seven years old, finally speak, was shocking for me. I was NOT calm, so much for not making an event of him speaking for the first time. I was overjoyed!

Ayale grew as any child would and often got into mischief which always had me clutching my heart. I know some people may think I was an over-protective Mom. I would agree. He was mine and I felt responsible for his care and whereabouts. I was so happy to be his Mother.

One Saturday evening I couldn't find Ayale. I know he was hiding somewhere in the house and so I went looking for him. I finally found him in the bathroom behind the shower curtain. He was standing in a puddle of blood and the scared look in his eyes was enough to break my heart. I looked in his hand and there was a razor which I used to shave my legs.

He often saw me shaving my legs in the bathroom. Somehow he found my razor and had decided to give himself a shave. I looked at his little feet and the right one had a line without skin from his ankle to his knee. He had pressed so hard on the razor it took the skin off his feet. He wasn't crying. I think he was more worried I was going to beat him for touching the razor in the first place. *How could I?* He had learnt a lesson and I too realized I should've put the razor completely out of his way. I turned the shower on, washed his leg then dressed the cut. When his Dad came home, I told him what happened, He thought it was funny. Ayale shaving his seven-year-old leg that had no hair. I was learning first-hand what being a mother meant.

We liked living in Montego Bay. It was a city, smaller than Kingston but seemingly huge in comparison to Port Antonio which was a one-street town. I began knitting again but this time deciding to create adult clothing instead of baby's since the market for adult garments was better, especially with the many tourists visiting Montego Bay.

Ian did the ground work by walking all over the city with samples of the things I made till he began getting orders. Our first order was from a woman working at the Sunshine Plaza named Christina Gonzales (Prout).

I would knit every day and night.

Knitting became like breathing for me and I was proud of every piece I completed. Quite soon, Ian got a shop at the Montego Cruise ship pier to order knitted tops for women from us. She was the only person at the complex to carry our line of knitted tops. It seemed I could not knit enough to fill the orders.

One night as I was trying to complete a top for Ian to deliver the following day, I fell asleep while knitting. Ian woke me and said I should check if I made any mistakes; he was speaking to me and got no response (he realized I had fallen asleep) but my knitting needles were still going. When I checked, it was perfect. I hadn't made any mistakes. He laughed and said that I was a super woman.

With the steady income from the knitting and Ian's one of a kind hand painted t-shirts, we were now able to fit Ayale with his second hearing aid.

Life started to get better for us. We were now able to eat properly and help to feed other children less fortunate than us. It seemed wherever we lived the children from the community always ended up at our home. I cannot recall a single child (or any children) in all of our years of raising Ayale, who had both parents raising or living with them in the same home. Mothers would often leave their children with us when they had errands to run. It seemed the best of both worlds for me, since, the children always came to our home to play and even eat - we would feed anyone at our home when we cooked - it meant Ayale always had children to play with and I was able to keep a watchful eye on them all.

Moving to Montego Bay was paying off for us and eventually we decided to open a little shop in the yard where we lived across from the school. Our rooms were behind a supermarket and there was a huge metal gate to the side. This was where we set up our bamboo shop and drew the sign Knit Fits on the gate.

After being open for a week we got a visit from a Rasta couple (Kibbibe and her husband). They purchased everything in our little shop and ordered more.

But living in a furnished, rented apartment was eating away at all our income and so we decided it was best to find an unfurnished place that we could move to and save to purchase a piece of land to build our dream home. We found a little one board room which was like a box - no bigger than twelve x twelve feet. We bought a bed, a small fan, a black and white 12 inch television and a small coal stove and moved up the road this time behind the Granville Post Office.

This was a community within the community.

Everyone was poor and we were the only ones with a television, with the bed in the room there was hardly space to turn around. At nights we would take the mattress off the divan, make a bed on the divan for Ayale and Ian and I would sleep on the mattress. But it seemed we were never alone. Children were always at our door and in the evenings would sit or stand on the steps to watch cartoons on the television. During the days Ian would sit on the chair by the door with a piece of board in his lap painting t-shirts and dresses which he sold.

Unearthing the Diamond

The woman who used to purchase the knitted tops from us had moved and so Ian was the sole breadwinner and he now had a customer at the Fantasy Hotel, Miss Beverly Haughton who would purchase whatever he painted.

Sometimes when I would complain that I didn't have the finer things in life Ian would remind me to look around at the amount of families we were helping including one girl Erica Morrison who we were sending to school. "Count your blessings Tamika. This is just a stop in the road for us. Look to the future."

I was very active in The Parent's Teachers Association at Ayale's school and was proud of him. His reading was below that for his age but his writing, math and drawing was above average. He made friends easily and was well behaved at school. He loved to draw and so we bought him drawing pads and provided him with paint sets and crayons.

He too looked to his Dad the way I did and because of his hearing aids and illness as a baby, I was an over-protective mother. He became my 'handbag' [1] and the only place he went without me was to school. Once he was home I would take him where ever I went. Sometimes I would make clothes for him but he never showed any interest in the sewing machine but would rush for his art books, paints or crayons to draw something to show his Dad.

Ayale was very active in school. It seemed he'd a lot of catching up to do. He did track, played cricket and football but no matter what he did he was most comfortable doing Art. At the age of nine, he was drawing full scale maps on chalk board for his class teacher and making his pocket money drawing on charts for other teachers. Though he now wore two hearing aids, the quality left a lot to be desired and even today, with digital hearing aide he's unable to hear certain letters or sounds. For example, he can't speak or hear the letter "c" (to this day he says a, b, t, d, e, f, g..., so the word 'cement' for him is 'tement').

This has not hindered him in the least and we raised him to know life owed him no favours. He attended

---

[1] Medical term - Dilatation and Curettage; it's a medical process used after a miscarriage to remove remnants after miscarriage from the uterus.

Unearthing the Diamond

Herbert Morrison Technical High School where his strongest subject was art and graduated from The Art Institute of Fort Lauderdale with a diploma in Graphic Desk Top Design. Today Ayale has an equal share holder in our family business an Eco Tourism Attraction located in Montego Bay. It's called: Ahhh...Ras Natango Gallery & Garden

Tamika Felina Pommells Williams

Hurricane Gilbert

On Sunday, September 11th, 1988, Ayale and I went to church and while there the pastor said there was a hurricane heading for Jamaica. I was 27 years old and had NEVER experienced a hurricane. As a young girl I grew up hearing about Hurricane Charlie which hit Jamaica in the early 50's and ever since, whenever a storm threatened to hit the island, the elders would say Jamaica is a God blessed country since the hurricane would seem to turn away without making landfall in Jamaica.

This was the sentiment of everyone at church and all over Jamaica that Sunday but the media tried to warn the people to be prepared but we all said the hurricane would pass us by.

On Monday morning September 12th, 1988, the entire island woke to the dreaded news. The hurricane had made landfall in Kingston and would be taking a direct tract across the entire island.

No one was prepared.

Unearthing the Diamond

Schools and businesses immediately closed but no one had stocked up on food, water or any supplies and now it was too late. All we could do was wait out the storm and pray it wasn't going to be as bad as they predicted.

As the morning went by, the skies grew black and there was an eerie silence. The radio went out as power lines and trees came crashing down. Ayale, who was nine-years-old, was frightened and we put him in his bed after he ate and told him it was ok and that he should go to sleep.

The wind was ferocious and I was scared. The room we lived in seemed to cry out as the wind and rain lashed it but finally Ayale fell asleep. Our little wooden room had a zinc roof and we were worried we would lose it but suddenly the wind and rain stopped and I breathed a sigh of relief. The hurricane came, passed us by and nothing had happened to our home. I opened the door but Ian said, 'Tamika DON"T it's not over."

"Look Ian, it's calm. There's no more rain and the wind has gone." I answered.

Tamika Felina Pommells Williams

He said one word, 'Tamika!"

It chilled me to the bone and I closed the door. No sooner had I done so the wind returned worst than before. Trees fell around the house and we stood by the little window and watched the roof from a nearby factory rip completely off and floated effortlessly away like a piece of paper. It sailed across the road, landing on the nearby playing field of the Sam Sharpe Teachers' College.

I was really scared and looked at Ayale but he was sound asleep. I was happy he was sleeping since I wouldn't know what to do if he had been awake.

But then our worst fear was realized as we heard the roof of our little room being ripped away. I started to cry and held onto Ian. The zinc roof was gone and some solitex (thin lining below the zinc roof) prevented us from seeing the sky. Water began to enter and we used buckets and wash pans to collect the water while making sure the bed stayed dry. Suddenly Ayale woke and started to cry. Ian went over to him and calmed him. I was shaking but needed to show Ian I was not a baby so I pretended to be strong. When the hurricane finally passed, leaving the island behind, it left complete chaos and devastation. When night finally came, we couldn't sleep and had to stay awake since thieves were using the darkness to loot and create more havoc.

It rained all night.

Tuesday September 13th, 1988, we went outside at the crack of dawn to see the destruction. Huge trees were on their sides and houses were completely flattened. We lost our roof and didn't have money to buy any new zinc to re-roof and neither did anyone else. We saw people ripping the sheets of zinc from the factory's roof which was laying in the playfield. Ian and I left Ayale at home and headed to the field and there we took enough sheets of zinc to redo our roof. We still had to take turns watching the sheets of zinc since there were so many families who needed the scarce resource.

It was painful to see the landscape, trees were either broken in half or completely up rooted, homes totally destroyed and there was no food. The woman Ian was supplying with his hand painted t-shirts requested some right away and he was the first person on the island to come out with a line of "I survived Hurricane Gilbert" T- shirts. This was our only source of funds during the clean up after the hurricane.

It was during that time, the resilience of the Jamaican spirit became evident as everyone began singing the song written and performed by Lloyd Lovindeer, "Wild Gilbert."

"Water come ina me room,

Me sweep out some wid di broom.

Di little dog laugh to see such sport and de dish run away with the spoon.

Uno se me dish Uno see me dish

Anybody uno see me satellite dish

Full a bully beef fulla bully beef.

Wah-wah-wah Wild GIlbert"

(c) Lloyd Lovindeer, Wild Gilbert, 1988

Everyone was singing the song because we all experienced what the song was about and since bully beef was the only meat available for weeks. The years post Hurricane Gilbert, saw Jamaicans making stronger home of concrete with concrete roofs.

Ian, Ayale and I had SURVIVED Hurricane Gilbert.

When the school reopened they had an emergency PTA meeting which I attended. It seemed after the hurricane many of the teachers with visas to the USA had gone away to work as domestic helpers since that paid better than the job of being a teacher and so there were classes without teachers. Since the school did not want to close till they could source more teachers they asked the parents to volunteer time to sit with a class till they could find trained teachers. Of course I volunteered and the first day I visited the Grade Four block, I saw there was no roof. The hurricane had ripped it off. I also knew the government wouldn't be able to assist immediately because this was just one classroom and there were so many schools across the island that couldn't even reopen because of how badly damaged they were.

I had an idea, we could do a fund raiser but when I told the principal, she said it had never been done before and wouldn't work. My idea was for the beauty pageant to give back to the school and children.

So I went out on my own, without the support of the school and approached the owner of the factory that had lost its roof with my idea. He loved it and suggested I would have to do the foot work in my own time but it could be done.

Ian assisted me as I planned the first ever Mimi Miss Granville, where girls between the ages of 7 and 9 were taught traditional Jamaican dance dialect and songs. I got sponsors for each girl and in the end had a total of 8 contestants.

It was amazing the response from the business places which made me feel proud and each one sponsored a girl with an evening dress, bouquet of flowers and a gift package. The Sam Sharpe Teachers' College offered us the use of their auditorium free of charge. The pageant was a success. It was covered by the local newspapers and the money turned over to the principal. With the

Unearthing the Diamond

money we raised, we were able to repair the Grade Four classroom roof.

I had found my calling.

And the principal along with a chief education officer Mrs. Waite–Reid (may she rest in peace) decided to send me to every teachers' seminar. One day, she remarked that some teachers were trained to be teachers while others were born teachers - she said I was a born teacher. After the first month of volunteering as a teacher, I was permanently employed as a pre-trained teacher.

I took my job seriously and dressed nicely yet comfortably for school and carried the air I got from my teachers when I went to primary/elementary school.

It was also natural for me to realise that many of the children I was teaching were hurting in so many different ways. A lot of them came to school hungry and dirty and I found myself buying a bag of Nutribun and milk each day[2]. I would provide the

---

[2] Bumboclatt' is a swear word in Jamaica but the shock of hearing him speak a full sentence was more than I could contain. The swear word was used in joy.

bun and milk I purchased the day before to my children whenever they complained of being hungry. I knew they needed to focus on their lessons since they couldn't learn on a hungry stomach.

Most of my colleagues, on the other hand, were trained teachers and didn't show a lot of interest in the children they taught, they would shout at the children in patois (broken English). But I realized something amazing; I was using my life experiences in my job. It helped me to identify children who were lacking parental love, children who were physically and sexually abused and children with learning disabilities.

I would come home and discuss different students with Ian who would give me suggestions on ways to help them and soon I was being more than a teacher to my class. I became their mother. I would interact with them during break on the playing field and congratulated them whenever they were early or mastered a task. I laughed with them and at them and they laughed with and at me when I acted silly. Here I was with children who used to come to class dirty and now they were all clean. If I didn't feel like playing at break-time my class would sit-in and we would all read stories or they would tell me about their lives at home.

They enjoyed coming to school and I enjoyed being a part of their lives. Because the classes were huge every afternoon we would hold discussions on general knowledge, where they would be placed into groups and dramatized the events happening to them and ways to resolve conflicts. This was most popular amongst them as they got to learn of ways of solving issues without violence.

I LOVED all my students and they loved me. I was not teaching a class of sixty students. I was teaching sixty individuals with different needs. Parents began visiting to inform me how well behaved and well spoken their child (ren) were and how happy they were I was the child's/ren's teacher. I used to be happy as a child when I went to school at their age and they were happy. I spent six years teaching at Granville All Age School. I taught Grades One and

Two for most of this time but was given Grade Four in my last year.

I had developed a reputation for working wonders with the most difficult children and the principal asked me to try with the Grade Four because they were unruly and caused a lot of trouble. Most of them were thought to have learning disabilities but none of them did, they were all only nine-year-olds expected to be adults with adult responsibilities at home. There was one boy who would ALWAYS sleep in class on a Monday. Only Mondays. When I enquired why, he wouldn't say. I let it go for a while. When I approached him again he finally told me that his mom had a man who visited on Sunday nights, they lived in one-room and he and his sister were locked out of the room which they shared with their mom so they just walked the streets till he left and then they would finally get to go to bed. I knew I couldn't relay this information to his Mom but I did meet with her. I told her how "bright" her son was and I was concerned that he often fell asleep in class. Her response shocked me:

Unearthing the Diamond

"Teacher! Dem fada lef me and me have a little man weh help me wid dem. Him married you know. So him come check me every Sunday night. Me caan mek dem stay in de room wid we teacher."

I asked, "Where do they go?"

"Teacher me tell dem fi go walk up an down, sometime all one a clock dem get fi go to dem bed."

I was sorry for her but knew this was her way of surviving and helping to feed her children. I didn't judge her. I just told her the children weren't safe on the streets till one a.m. and needed proper rest before coming to school. I promised I would allow her son to sleep in the staff room for a couple of hours on Monday mornings till she figured a way.

Her son only slept in the staff room once because the following Monday he announced to the entire class: *"Me sleep so good last night. Me mother get a job at Freeport and left de fool fool man."*

We all laughed.

Because Ayale had not spoken until he was over seven-years-old, I was able to help parents who had children with learning disabilities. Ian became my encyclopedia. He would help me research behaviour in children and got me books to read about children with special needs. I was able to identify some children from the books I read and applied some suggestions which worked.

I became the envy of the teachers who began to badmouth me.

They started saying I was just a pre-trained teacher who hadn't acquired the formal education and was behaving as if I was more intelligent than them. They even said all I did was play with the kids and the kids weren't learning a thing from me. I was devastated. I knew some of what they said was true, I wasn't formally trained but I had worked and applied myself more than anyone else on staff. Even the Education Officer who came to access the school, Mrs. Waite Reid, would tell the principal how much she admired my class and that the other teachers should follow my lead with teaching aids and so on.

Once, I remember going home to cry on Ian and told him I was not going back to school the next day. Ian was adamant: *"You can't just run away he said because the battle is heating up. What did you expect? That they would all love you for showing them up?"*

But I wasn't trying to show any one up, I just wanted to make sure I was informed about what I was teaching and wanted to learn with the children. That was it, I was there teaching these children but was learning too, I was learning from them as well as educating myself. The very questions I'd ask Ian when he was explaining a problem to me was how I was preparing to teach them and respond correctly whenever they asked me. Ian would say to me: *"Don't just take my word for it Tamika, look it up. You cannot afford to give them even the tiniest error. You HAVE to be correct at all times."*

I think because I thought like a child I didn't think myself above them and so I was able to reach and teach them in the language they understood. This difficult Grade Four with under achievers surprised everyone. And at the end of the school year I decided to quit teaching because they were now able to move to Grade Five and I was scared of getting a new set of children since it broke my heart to let these go. We became a family and even today when I see them on the road I know each one by their full names and they'll affectionately tell me: *"Teacher, you ah me BEST teacher ever."*

They were my best students ever and thanks to Hurricane Gilbert I found my calling as a teacher which would span over 22 years of my life.

I'd found my calling and I looked forward to going to school everyday. I spent time with the parents, sharing ways of staying in tune with what was happening with their children and I felt I was making a difference. One year I remembered having over eighty students in my class. The children were seven-year-olds. It seemed nothing could be taught in the academics with this many students but I found a way and we spoke a lot and the light bulbs would slowly but surely go off in their head. They loved coming to school and I was happy.

Unearthing the Diamond

You know, I'd no plans to be a teacher. It just happened and I found out I became a student in the school of life, even though I was paid to teach these children.

In the government school's, the children were at such a disadvantage with overcrowded classrooms and overworked teachers who weren't passionate about teaching or the well-being of the students. To them it was just a job. I witnessed teachers selling snacks to students during class time as well as break time and even the way some dressed for the job was appalling. Then after my sixth year as a pre-trained teacher, I began teaching in private schools and used all the methods I employed at the Granville All Age School.

The Deokoro Magnet for the Gifted and Talented was my first experience in a private school.

There were small classes of no more than ten students and suddenly I was able to teach each child individually. Hands on, research, reading books, supplies, everything a teacher needed to enhance a child's teaching experience was available. Then one day, I had an important revelation: *'children were the same no matter their colour age or financial standing of their parents'.*

My experience in the government school's showed me the lack of love and attention the children there had. Many came from single parent homes with the mother who had multiple children as the sole bread winner. But when in private schools, I saw the same need for attention and affection in the "rich" children.

The cost of attending a private pre/prep school in Montego Bay was comparable to some tertiary institutions and locally if a child/ren attended a private school it would be referred to as the "rich kid's school".

The children in private schools where I taught needed as much attention and sometimes more as the 'poorer' children. Their parents were so busy with making money that raising their children became a job for the teachers. Then there were the activities after school. Children left home at 7:00 a.m., were driven to school by parent, nanny or guardian; spent all day at school then would've two, sometimes three after-school activities to attend. This meant some children were at school for at least twelve hours. They then have homework and eight hours sleep which leaves three hours with their parents. These were the same children who were sent away for holidays.

I knew there had to be a middle ground. Our job as parents and educators was to enable and prepare children to function within society and every institution whether "government or private" had its pros and cons. I've lived and taught in all them. The children were crying out:"teach us, show us the way, spend some time with us, and speak to us".

Being an educator has brought me so many insights into life.

It had been another difficult time for me but I learnt not to run away but stand and fight.

This part of my life is another book in itself and so I close this chapter giving thanks to a hurricane that came and in so many ways and 'helped' so many people. From people building stronger homes to the lives of the thousands of children I taught, hopefully, positively touching their lives.

Unearthing the Diamond

Ahhh...Ras Natango Garden & Gallery

Ian always promised we would eventually purchase a piece of land in the hills overlooking the ocean. He had a love for seeing the ocean and as an artist needed to have a view. I often thought this would never happen since we were just getting by.

After Hurricane Gilbert, we were given notice to leave the one-room we rented and this time Ian insisted we needed to stop moving from place to place; it was time for us to settle down as a family. He said he was looking for land to buy. I didn't want to burst his bubble and wondered what were we going to purchase the land with?

He visited a few communities searching for land but couldn't find anything that suited his desires. One day he left home on his search and this time took a friend by the name of Michael (Muggins) with him. He said he felt that this was the day. Ayale and I waited patiently for their return.

Later that day when they did return Ian was beside himself. He'd found the perfect place and said,

"Tamika everything worked like clockwork. I found a piece of land and paid JA$3,000 to hold the land."

I didn't share Ian's excitement because I knew we didn't have the money to pay for land and all we had was $5,000 an he just paid out $3,000 of it. I tried not to show any fear and said I'd like to see it.

The next day we went to view the property.

It was like a forest but when I turned around and saw the view I was completely sold. I asked Ian how was it possible that the owner had agreed to take only $3,000 to mark the land and he said, "Everything aligned perfectly. She was having a cashflow problem and needed cash and this was a way out for her."

The three of us (Ian, the landowner and I), went to an attorney and made arrangements to pay the remainder of the cost of the land, and with hard work and the financial help from friends, we were able to complete payment on the land. It took us over three years to finally pay for the land. The agreement was we would make incremental payments.

Unearthing the Diamond

Everyone in the community laughed at us when we finally got the property cleared. I loved planting vegetables and flowers but this land was covered with nothing but stones and rocks. And on a steep hillside.

Ian was not to be deterred. He drew the design and told me where the house would go. He said the driveway would go over there; tank up there, pool over there, the garden over there and on and on. I would've preferred to wait until we saw the money all at once to do any building but he was a man with a plan and obviously on a mission. I never told him my fears and pretended to see all he was telling me.

We rented an old house close to the property and began building. It took us six years to complete a part of the house to move in and did we pay our dues in this new community and learnt the hard way. Ian made all the decisions and decided to use workmen from the area instead of bringing in people from outside. But the very persons we paid to work on building our house and even the watchman stole so much from us.

Tamika Felina Pommells Williams

One month I collected my salary from school and we used it to purchase zinc for the roofing. After it was delivered, they were all stolen along with the lumber for the floor. I loved wooden floors since I had wooden floors as a child in my grandparents' home.

And through all this, I still couldn't understand how Ian could stay so calm or find something positive in every situation. He was upset that they stole our material since he wanted to help provide employment but he had had enough and fired all the workmen, bringing in new ones from outside the community.

Ian decided we would change the design of the house and would make the floors and roof out of concrete, he said this would make the house more stable and be able to withstand a hurricane.

Finally, though, the stress took its toll on Ian and he collapsed at the airport on our way back from a holiday to the USA. When we reached the hospital, he needed immediate surgery as he had a perforated ulcer. I was scared out of my wits but happy when he pulled through. He recovered when we were able to finally move into our home he was overjoyed

Unearthing the Diamond

Ian was a man on a mission. Some of the things we had endured would've broken any other typical man but Ian was no typical man. Not with the so many setbacks while building our home on the edge of a cliff. I remember the laughter and jeers from community members as they said we were swindled out of our money since nothing could be done with this piece of land. I recalled an old lady stating: "poor Ian," one day when she saw us heading to the land.

Within Jamaica there were so many things which we use to tear each other down. One of the things we were frequently told was, "Uno no come from yah so. Uno come from town, go back wey uno come from."

These words hurt but Ian maintained, "We are Jamaicans and have a right to live wherever we choose to in our island."

Building on builder-friendly land had its challenges let alone building on a cliff in the mountain. The first construction was the water tank and even today we have no running water, so every household has to provide its own water supply. Most people do their washing at the spring in the neighbouring community of Gutters, using for cooking and drinking. Ian chose the location of the water tank at the highest point of the land," so gravity fed the house," he said.

The back-wall of the house was completed and even then I couldn't visualize a home on the mountainside. The wall stayed there for a couple of years and when we finally resumed construction there was another set of problems.

As the construction of our home seemed to be coming to a close, the workmen began dragging their feet and kept pushing back our moving in deadline set by Ian; each week the payout kept going up.

I remembered one Friday before making payment to the contractor, Ian had him measure and mark each wall so as not to keep paying for the same job over and over. This worked and each week the payment seemed more reasonable. Everything was almost ready with the windows and doors waiting to be installed. Ian gave the builder one week for completion but by the end of the week - nothing - so we hired a truck and moved in while they hurriedly installed all the windows and doors. I couldn't believe it, the workmen had dragged out completing our home so that they could keep getting paid but finally it was over and we were able to settle in.

I loved the view from our new home but hated the property there was nowhere to walk since it was covered with solid rock, loose stones and boulders. One day I suggested to Ian for us to sell the stones. His response was a simple *'No'*. He said we could terrace the land as they did in Asia. I thought he was mad. He set about making the terraces and soon after we employed labourers to assist in completing the project.

Suddenly, another problem arose.

No soil, so again I suggested to Ian, "Let's purchase a load of top soil and spread on the rocks he had arranged into beds?"

But Ian said no. It seemed Ian always said no to me but his reasons were valid. No truck could make it up the steep track to our home and we couldn't afford to pay labourers to transport a truckload of soil a bucket at a time.

Tamika Felina Pommells Williams

So he said, "We shall compost."

We now have a world renown garden and after over 28 years still compost, replenishing each bed annually. Still a work in progress but the challenges have made our home a special place for us as well as our guests who choose to visit our attraction.

In a single sentence Ian stated, "Bloom where you are planted."

We were finally able to create a wonderful home in the mountains, overlooking Montego Bay. We now live over two thousand feet above sea level, twenty minutes from Sam Sharpe Square, the centre of the city; up in the mountains where your ears may pop on the drive up the hill. Our community is small and peaceful and during the hot summer months we sleep with our windows open. We live on half acre of land. It took us over twenty years to get it to where it is today and is still a work in progress but it is comfortable and our home. We have the most amazing view of Montego Bay, more than two hundred and twenty degrees of unimpeded view of the city and the landscape changes at night as we watch the city come to life with its glowing lights. The magic happens even more so after a shower of rain, when it washes the air and cause the city's lights to twinkle.

There is a magic in our home and when people arrive, they don't want to leave.

Our home was built with the lay of the land and the stones and rocks turned into terraces that hold the soil in our gardens - flower beds, herb and vegetable garden and my favourite: a fantasy garden.

As environmentalists, it broke our heart when we were forced to cut a huge tree at the end of the property that was at least one hundred years old. It started showing signs that the huge branches were beginning to become hollow and we were afraid that should it fall it would tear up the land around it, so we cut it, and used the lumber to make the spiral stairway inside our home and the many benches in the garden. The root system of the tree rose majestically to at least seven feet above the ground. I didn't want to remove it, so Ian suggested creating a fairy garden within its roots.

Ayale got busy and created houses for the fairies using the bark of the tree for the roofs. We made a well and landscaped the fantasy garden with miniature plants. The houses are out in the open but are easily overlooked. There are fairies beside the houses and the Queen fairy sits at the foot of the village in what we created as the swimming hole.

It is by far the most relaxing part of the garden for me.

We collect pieces of our history and these are evident throughout the garden. Old wrought iron pots, a piece of slave chain, Tilly lamps and wooden sculpture from cedar roots. A huge rock that we could not break was transformed by Ian into a great white shark. With our many flowers, we have attracted all types of birds including Jamaica's National Bird - the Scissors Tail-Humming bird.

We have birds that migrate here every winter to enjoy our garden. A small fish and turtle tank is also on the property. The only thing that isn't here yet is the pool but in time it will come to fruition.

Unearthing the Diamond

The latest addition to our home is our gallery: Ahhh...Ras Natango Gallery and Garden Tour.

In an attempt to heal myself I unconsciously created a piece of paradise, a place of beauty, tranquility, peace and a place to meditate.

Tamika Felina Pommells Williams

Empowerment

I go back to the beginning.

Growing up without my parents especially my mother helped me to make some decisions about myself as a mother and wife. From a small child I had decided I would NEVER abandon my children no matter what the circumstances or difficulties. I hold no ill will towards my mother for making her choices. She was from a family of professionals and it must've seemed to her siblings that she was throwing her life away and it was their decision to send her to England for a better life and to escape from my father who was physically abusive to her. Her father (Dad - my grandpa) was a little boy on a slave plantation in Clarendon and here was my mom "shacking up" with a married man and worse yet a white married man.

You must understand the culture of the times. Most families could only send one child to school and it was usually the one who they thought was "bright", having a mixed child was seen as a blessing since more opportunities would open up to a child with light complexion. My Dad sired forty-three children and he was married, most of the women had two children, my Mom was the only woman who had three children for him. The women of that era didn't care if the white man or light skin man supported their children since all they cared about was the offspring who would have a light complexion and what they called, "pretty hair." My mother was most likely the envy of her peers since she was the mother of not one, not two but four light-skinned children.

This history was a part of being descendants of slaves, where we were conditioned to believe our dark skin was a hindrance.

Today women with my complexion are called "browning" and now both women and men have been using various chemicals on their skin to get a lighter complexion. This is an epidemic in Jamaica. Not only of our legacy from slavery but the dangers to the skin, killing the natural melanin which protects us from the sun. With my lighter complexion and as I age, I have begun to have numerous dark spots on my face which darker shinned women in my age group do not have.

Tamika Felina Pommells Williams

When Mom moved to England and our aunt took us to live with our grandparents, they must've overlooked the fact their Dad was a slave boy whose mother, Nana Blake was a cook to Backra Massa. The tables were now turned since Grandpa now had a white man's children working for him; and worked us he did. I had no knowledge of any of this when I was growing up, otherwise than feeling abandoned but even when I did acquire the knowledge, I wouldn't have left my children to the mercy of others.

The feeling of low self esteem was overwhelming as a child and I felt abandoned. *How can I explain the feeling of not having a mother for myself?* I'd look at other families and dreamt that my mother would wake up one day and decide to return to us. I was lucky in many ways because her parents took care of us and gave us a good home with harsh discipline but a good home nonetheless. So when I had my son I decided to never allow him to experience the emptiness of not having me in his life. All the things I lacked growing up I made sure they were available for him even when it meant I had to sacrifice or literally go without. I desperately wanted to be responsible for helping to make the world a better place and I thought I could do this through my son.

Ian was always the voice of reason and felt Ayale had a grounded childhood between his Dad and I. Being a woman who experienced first hand the ugliness of men and boys to a young girl, I decided to make sure my son would **never** take a woman by force so taught him to be gentle, loving and considerate. It was a form of brainwashing since it was not so much by what I said but the way I acted. I was always the peacemaker at home, at school and within the community. If there was a problem with Ayale and his friends I would always get them to talk it out and he would always come to me if he had a problem and needed help solving it.

I sheltered him and now as I write realised the wrong I did to my own son. I raised him based on my experiences and that was not right for him. The pressure I must've placed on him I swear was **NOT** intentional. I just wanted him to have the life I never had and to never lack the emotional support I so desperately needed. This process of healing was now uncovering things I did and I thought was for the best. Now I'm not so sure.

I never trusted anyone.

I don't have many friends and I now realize my son was raised that way too. All the friends he had when he was going to school always visited him at home and I ensured he had all the games and toys they would want to play with. Most weekends he and his friends would be at my home as I told myself it was better since the other boy's parents knew they were safe with us and I *knew* Ayale was at home.

I'd cook for them and met all their moms who visited our home at least once. They came to find out if their children were comfortable and safe. I know I may sound over-protective but this was what occurred to me when I looked at it in a different light. I didn't want my son to ever experience the darkness I felt as his mother and I needed to protect him from pain and disappointment that was sure to come.

I remember when he started attending high school and would stay behind to watch the football matches; this meant he'd get home a bit after dark.

Unearthing the Diamond

Naturally, I would be beside myself with worry and every vehicle passing our home and stopped, I would be looking out to see if it was him coming home. His Dad would tell me to stop because it would upset Ayale. So I would hide on the veranda and when Ayale was dropped by a taxi, he wouldn't know I had been waiting.

Ian would say, "Tamika you have to learn to let him go. Trust him. As long as we don't get a phone call, don't worry."

Even if he went to the movie with a girl, I wouldn't go to sleep and stay up while Ian went to bed. It was only when the dogs announced Ayale's arrival, would I quickly turn off the lights and head to bed before he enter the house. I knew Ian was right but couldn't help myself. I needed to protect Ayale at all costs even if it meant not going to sleep until he got home. I spent all my life thinking I was the best mom but now, looking back, I saw how I stifled my son's growth and I am *angry*.

I am angry because I didn't get the professional help I needed and though Ian tried, I am still amazed how even he stayed with me. I also needed to feel that the experiences I had would somehow be good for my son, my husband and other persons who have gone through sexual abuse just like I have. Girls who go through it since as a society we still condone and allow it to happen while it's hidden away having a far reaching impact on the wellbeing of the families it affects. Women and girls are preyed upon by older men and spend the rest of their lives trying to maintain their sanity. I personally survived it because I wore so many masks. There were times when I was overwhelmed and the feeling of being not good enough, being tarnished. I felt I always had to make things right for everyone, be perfect for people to accept and love me, making sure I was good at whatever I did. I could not take being the butt of a joke or being disliked. What other people thought of me was more important than anything else in my life. Being brutally raped affected my life in so many ways and for thirty years I couldn't say the word rape aloud. I couldn't watch movies where women were being sexually abused. I even hated seeing romantic movies and hid my own sexuality and to this day unable to enjoy being kissed. They robbed me of my youth, my sexuality, my self esteem, my self confidence and my freedom. As such I have used my husband as an excuse and a crutch. He was my protector and still is and I never go anywhere alone at nights to this day. I can't travel in a taxi with more men than women and dread that my husband may one day wake up and wonder why he put up with me and this damn baggage I have carried for so long.

How could I tell these people how much they've affected my life?

Society tends to blame the woman for being raped, either she is dressed too sexily, led him on or in my case, trusted him. The system is then set up to work against the woman, making her feel like she was the perpetrator rather than the victim and in this way most women prefer to hide the fact that a complete and unwanted invasion of their body took place.

Sexual assault affects the victim on so many levels. First, it's the invasion of one's body against their will, the emotional baggage that follows. Then, the social isolation and stigma while trying to survive and function as a member of a family and society.

Self blame is also very real. For me, *how could I've allowed this to happen?* If only I hadn't stayed behind to attend that stupid sewing class. If only I'd listened to my intuition telling me I may not be safe. If only my feet worked and I ran when I know I could've, even though there was no escape. Why had my body shut down and froze, causing me not to even scream. W*hy had I survived this assault?* These and many more unanswered questions made me feel I was the one who caused this and no matter how I was told differently, it simply ate away at me. *How could I rebuild myself when I had been rendered completely naked? How long does this journey take?*

The first line of defense was survival.

Without even knowing I'd gone into survival mode, my body found unusual ways to protect me. Our bodies try to heal but in truth there were no set rules, at least not for me on what that healing looked or felt like.

Unearthing the Diamond

Foremost in my mind was getting clean; washing the images away from my mind, body and soul but no matter how I washed myself the pain was still there. I never felt clean .The images stayed in my mind and the simple things would trigger them with all the work I've done suddenly disappearing as the fear took center stage once more. The best line of defense for me was the many masks I created and wore. I hide my feelings, fears, uncertainties, pain and frustrations cleverly behind all these different masks and people never knew.

They'd look at me and say how confident I was, how self assured but I would smile and wished they looked into my eyes. Yes, I wore these masks quite well. The Professional Mask.

Once, I remembered cleaning one the homes where we lived. There were times when Ian would sit in a chair and as soon as he got up, I straighten the cushions. If he walked in and a piece of leaf dragged in after him, I would be behind him with a broom. One day he turned around and said, "Tamika we live here. This is not a show room, it's our home. It's ok to be messed up at times."

I really wanted to explain to him that in moments when I compulsively clean were the times I was trying to stay calm. I wore masks even with Ian because I knew he would feel helpless if I told him the many times I was down and devastated by the images in my mind and so when he mentioned about me cleaning too much I just said I was sorry and with that little word he would look at me and somehow he knew I was cleaning because it was my way to stay sane. Cinderella mask.

There were times when the depression was so unbearable I'd stay in bed, to stay and feel dirty. One December, about five years ago when I just couldn't shake the pain in my soul, Ian was upset because he thought I'd found a way to cope and here I was upset and him feeling the brunt of my anger. I literally cried for days, didn't eat, stayed in my room and I didn't come out for anything. I didn't bathe or use the bathroom except to pee. I kept the windows closed and curtains drawn, locking myself away.

Unearthing the Diamond

I just wanted to die again, for some reason. My sudden bout of depression was so intense and this after twenty-five years after the incident. After a couple of days, Ian was unable to take it anymore and came into the room and said, "Tamika, you're being too hard on yourself. I know what's wrong and it's ok. I know it's the anniversary of the attack and I understand."

Somehow I'd gone into a depressed state, completely unconsciously, on the date I was attacked and I didn't even realize it. I still couldn't will myself out of my bedroom and so went downstairs, took a tin of paint, returned and repainted it. When I finished, I put a border of flowers (wall paper) around the ceiling, I changed the curtains. Eventually, I was forced to leave the room because I was sick of the paint smell.

Because I literally starved myself for days, I could only drink a cup of tea and crackers that first day then gradually I started to eat again. (Without a mask)

I still don't know what I'd done to deserve being raised without my parents. What I'd done to those men and boys. I often asked myself if they ever thought about how they invaded and hurt me, changing the course of my life. *Don't they have sisters and mothers? How is it that I had to spend so much of my life carrying the shame of what they'd done to me and they went on with theirs? What had I ever done to any of you?* No human deserved to be abused the way you all abused me.

Something must be done.

I know it maybe too late for me and I must learn to continue to live with this but something must be done to prevent this happening here in Jamaica and all over the world. For so many years I was worried about my pain and my self-esteem but I received the following email from a man who attended the school at the time of the incident and because nobody took action it happened over and over and still happens. It MUST stop. (The names have been changed).

Copied from Facebook after sending the pages up to here to Vivian:

Unearthing the Diamond

"Wow, Tamika,

Your story is a powerful one that gripped me; I could not put it down, until I finished it on Tuesday. I can't wait to read the rest. I have a few suggestions and notes and I will send that to you soon but the story is such an uplifting one that it has to be told, and retold. I love Ian; he is all that I and I as brethren strive to be. I like the fact that you showed his human qualities, frailties' and all, but you also show his great strength and ambition to forge ahead in the art of survival and most importantly, his gentle and kind Rastafarian spirit. You needed to do this book in order to heal and my classmates and the world need to revisit this story which is repeating itself today, over and over. I am sure that some will draw strength from it and feel less alone in this somewhat cruel world we live in.

The XLCR part of it.

I am aware of this having taken place at school and I for one know it did happen. I am not sure of all who were involved but I remember it being talked about by one of the participants who were there. He was ashamed of his actions that evening and he cried as he talked about how he should have tried to rescue you but he said they were like a bunch of mad wolves that night. He was a member of the football team. I am very disturbed at the behavior of Mr. Wong; I will never see him in the same light again. I actually know of other girls who went through the same ordeal at least three come to mind readily and I wonder how they are doing in life right now and if they have gotten a chance to heal as you have.

My mom died last Monday night, so I am preparing her funeral rites and that has taken up a lot of my time, but I am as alright as can be (smile).

May Jah bless you and your family, will talk soon.

Vivian"

Never in all my years of this ordeal had it ever occur to me that there would be others. I'd been writing this book and was wondering how I was going to thank Ian for rescuing me, giving me a chance, for accepting me broken as I was and helping to rebuild me from scratch. And after I read Vivian's email, I realized, I'd been thanking Ian without planning to do so. I said I was writing my life story but Ian and I intertwine so much it was inevitable that Vivian would see Ian in my words.

I decided to raise my son in order to make a change and believed that women were raising their sons in a double standard kind of way. I had to raise my son differently. Being an only child he was exposed to everything his Dad and I did. He was taught to cook, wash, iron, sew and clean. He learned to carry a hundred pound bag of cement, learned to do carpentry and his calling art. These were the things he saw his Dad doing and thus no job was designated as a woman's or a man's.

He learned firsthand from his Dad how to treat a woman and whenever he had girlfriends round, he'd pull out their chair, walk the garden and just be a 'gentle' man with them. He's handsome and I thought with him being a 'gentle' man he'd have no difficulty in finding a woman to share his views, his life partner. But it seemed many girls only wanted to be disrespected and took his gentleness for weakness. His Dad told him not to settle for less or change his values as the right woman was out there for him and he would find her and she him.

It seemed I was trapped at the age of fifteen and used my teenage emotions to stay in tune with whatever was going on with Ayale. I made sure he never felt neglected and smiled as I recalled when he first began going through puberty.

I was teaching at Granville All Age where he was a student and I always said to him he could speak with me about anything - we were more like brother and sister than mother and son and one morning he said to me, "Mom at nights when I wake up my pants are wet."

I thought he meant he was wetting his bed so told him to make sure he peed before going to bed at nights. He laughed and said, "Mom I don't mean that. You said I should talk to you when this happened."

I was so shocked I just said, "When we get home your Dad will speak to you."

Unearthing the Diamond

This is a topic I spoke to my students about but when my own son came to me I was unable to speak with him. Slowly, he was becoming a man and that evening as soon as I got home I spoke with his Dad who in turn spoke with Ayale. Throughout the years Ayale learned the topics I was uncomfortable talking about and would go directly to his Dad and if there were things he wanted his Dad to know but didn't feel comfortable telling him, he'd come to me. He knew his Dad and I shared everything and this seemed a perfect way for Ian and I to stay abreast with what was happening in Ayale's life.

I took the back seat always to my husband and son and would go without in order for them to have. I know it sounds holier than thou but I felt they were more worthy than I and deserved better and so tried to make sure they'd always need me. *What a burden for both the men in my life?* So I hoped they too would never see through the masks I wore.

To all I seemed the perfect wife and mother but deep inside I was scared, uncertain of what to do but I was a quick learner and grasped things easily, mastering the art of being someone else but the giving of myself completely used to upset Ian who said I was over generous. He often would quote a Jamaican saying when he was frustrated with my kindness: *"Yuh going toh give away yuh ass and shit chue yuh ribs."*

I enjoyed giving even when I had nothing to give. I would put on birthday parties for both Ian and Ayale and invite their friends but wouldn't do the same for myself. The first birthday party I ever had was when I turned forty and Ian said it was a milestone and it had to be celebrated.

I didn't feel worthy and so I made sure did everything but today I realize that I am worthy and it's full-time for me to accept that I am indeed worthy. I've spread a lot of joy to others and though I felt good spreading these joy and gifts, it's ok to allow others to spread joy and gifts to me too. I know I'm a work in progress and that everything I did for my family was out of the goodness of my heart.

In writing this book I am casting away most of my masks. I'd like to say I'm casting away all of them but I'm taking this one step at a time and I'd be so hard on myself if I said I could cast them all away, then find myself still wearing one. I'm aware that in telling my story I'm opening doors that'll have consequences, however I cannot hide this any longer, and I refuse to protect anyone. Today, it's about me and my family. I'm aware some of the men who abused me might be settled in roles as fathers and husbands and their families may not be as understanding as we'd like to think but I cannot protect them anymore. My silence now would mean I'm sending a message that this type of brutality was and is acceptable.

A friend suggested I change the names in my book as some may want to sue me but I cannot in all fairness protect anyone, not even myself. I'm putting my life story out there and everyone will now know and draw their own conclusion and I will **not** protect any of those men. My response to the wives, mothers, sisters and daughters of these men would be simply this. I share because I haven't recovered from this experience and it has affected the relationship I'd like to have with the man who I have been married to for over 28 years. There are still times when we're making love and something triggers a negative reaction in me. I try not to let it show but being sensitive, he knows immediately. He would cuddle me and say, "It's ok, Tamika."

No matter how I told him nothing was wrong, he'd simply add, "Not in that light, I don't want you to ever see me in that light." Then he withdraws and we just cuddle.

Do you enjoy kissing your husbands? I've been married and living with Ian for over 32 years and I cannot kiss my husband. I cannot bear being touched by strangers and this was all a result of being brutally raped by someone's current husband. So should I still protect them? I say No! I've to let this out in the open, so I'm free, so I can open the eyes of women, parents, teachers, principals, friends and families.

When someone dies we grieve, then get on with our lives. When a woman gets raped she never gets over it, she hides and it affects every aspect of her life going forward. So, if I can help just one woman who

Unearthing the Diamond

shared my experience, help her to feel better about her life and help her to get help. If I can help a young girl to get help **now** and not allow it to consume her as it has me. If I can't be a whole woman at the end of this, then I would've written this and it would not been written for something.

The past, the present and the future.

The following inserts were between a schoolmate, Vincent, and me. I can't believe he decided to send me something about the past but I guess it was perfect timing.

Vincent: *"God has been good to us and we have the opportunity to dream/be/become all that God has created us to be...For some of us (probably all of us) the PAST is a real issue. For the upcoming year, please relinquish some stuff.... (I call this forgiveness, whether it's someone or something), let it go... if you do you'll be released to go forward"*...He goes on to speak about a schoolmate who used to train with weights on his ankles then relinquished them on sports day...*"Failures, mistakes, hurts, disappointments of the past are just that. They are the* past." He goes on to add. *"We have no 'now' and we have no future because we are prisoners of our past. Wise is the man and (woman too) who relinquishes the failures of yesterday (the past) for the dreams and hopes of today and tomorrow."*

I read this twice before responding.

Why had Vincent suddenly sent this to me and I'm at this chapter in my book dealing with the past. I wanted to say **never** would I ever forgive but I decided to respond when wearing one of my masks.

My reply: *"Vincent, I hear your sentiments but I beg to differ! There is NO future without a past! I do agree that we should move ahead and not dwell on past hurts but the past does shape who we are today and even tomorrow. I have chosen to see the positives in all my experiences; however I have LEARNED that without negative experiences we can never truly experience the stress free life we all crave. I refuse to forget my past! I am who I am despite my past! I just plain AM! I could go on forever but I have a future which is bright and must go cook dinner peace. Tamika*

Unearthing the Diamond

I thought that was the end of the discussion but alas there was a new correspondence from Vincent: *"If you look in the script that I wrote I made the analogy of wearing weights (I said failures etc.) and I think I said we use these to make ourselves better. I give you one example that I know of. It was a mother who lost her daughter, after that one event she stopped living. After a while she just stopped. Then she just died, No cause, no reason, I have been to the grave side of mothers who have lost daughters. They cried, held the coffin, etc. but they went on with their lives. I know they will never forget but they go on with life. I cant judge that other mother who died for I have not lost any of my children. But if something happen to anyone of us and we allow it, it has the possibility to stop us if we don't relinquish it. That was what I was basically saying. From what you said to me, we both agree. I think you think I was saying that we should "forget all our past. Tamika we are a collection of our past. You may think you disagree with me but we are on the same page."*

Tamika Felina Pommells Williams

This was too good to be true. The very things I wanted to say in my book I was not writing to Vincent. My response:

"It's amazing you chose the New Year to write about the past. I did read and understood all you wrote but I felt inclined to voice my opinions because unlike me many persons with painful pasts for one reason or another had no support and so they gave up. Many times in my life I wanted to give up but my husband refused to let me. Like Footprints in the sand he helped me to see that I was not alone but was being carried in the Master's hands. The past is very much A PART OF WHO WE ARE BUT I AGREE WE SHOULD not ALLOW IT TO CONSUME US. Some things happen to us when we are younger and weren't equipped with the necessary tools to cope so in order to survive we just file them away and move on. This form of escapism accomplishes only one thing. We unconsciously repeat actions which forces us to deal with the original problem from our past. So what do we do? We file it away yet again and the cycle just keeps repeating itself. We miss out on so many of life's pleasures and even simple things from nature

and love from our families because we find it hard to love ourselves. I speak in the third person. I believe I have done all the above like so many others but I AM healing myself. Some actions are easier to forgive and come to terms with. I have carried being brutally raped at fifteen by thirteen men and boys some of whom attended my school. I wanted to kill myself many times but somehow I survived. I am just learning to look back at that experience from my past which has affected me in so many ways, negative as well as positive. I am a good wife, mother and friend. I am good at what I do. I am an excellent teacher but the person within is still that fifteen year old girl who still aches and asks why? I am able to tell when my students are abused, are sexually active, in need of help because I experienced it all and able to identify the signs others would overlook. I have been able to help many of my students. So though they tried to break me I turned it around and took my life back. I have surrounded myself with beauty in order to stay sane because of the amount of ugly experiences from my past. What I really should have said yesterday in my response was that not all persons have support and without the support to help us stay focused and look past the thorns to see and smell the roses we just prick our fingers on the thorns and kiss our teeth as we curse the rose bush. I have roses in my garden so I see past the thorns literally. I did learn to debate at Excelsior for the three years I was there. Can you imagine if I had graduated? I am not crying over spilt milk. I am happy with who I am. Tamika"

Unearthing the Diamond

From Rocks to Paradise

Sitting on our porch overlooking the city below I am forced to give thanks, with all the experiences I've had I wonder if this was indeed my life? A husband who loves me, a handsome young man for my son that when I look at him I see how mature he has become and just how much he is like his father. He respects and knows himself. And in his soft gentle way, he can melt me with this one word: "Mom."

When we bought this bit of land to build our home in 1988, I never thought it would be what it is today. The little fifteen-year-old girl has grown up. No longer afraid of the world, no longer hiding behind her husband and no longer pretending she was strong. No need for pretense that she was a strong woman. Today, the little girl, a grown woman was ready to heal, ready to experience all she has created around her. I won't pretend that this has been an easy fix. It hasn't. I won't even pretend I have been fixed but I do know that I have been compressed, chiseled, shaped and polished. This lump of coal that was a little girl. An abandoned child. An abused child. This lump of coal tossed back into the earth until a miner came and unearthed it. One time, I felt useless, I felt I didn't deserve this man who insisted I had value.

Now that the diamond has been unearthed, my husband achieved his objective. I'm now confident in making my own decisions, for our business and family. I'm the one who worked at trying to repay this man, this angel, this super-being who believed in me and saw me when I couldn't see myself. He used to say: "Tamika, you don't give yourself enough credit. I did nothing. You had it buried in you and I just helped to bring it to light."

I can still hear him saying, "You can lead a horse to water but you cannot make it drink."

I can be a very difficult and stubborn woman and he used subtle ways in which to build my self confidence. I have days when I'm confident and days when I wear a mask. I'm learning to forgive myself as I forgive all the people who've hurt me. My life was different I must admit, I've been humbled and still have the scars from being sexually assaulted but I no longer allow my abusers the power of dictating

Unearthing the Diamond

whenever I'm not happy or to steal my joy. My happiness comes not from family and friends. It comes from within. When I'm in my garden I'm the happiest person alive and when my husband and son are happy, this thrills my soul. I may sound as if I worship my husband, I do not but I'm loyal to him because without his guidance my life would've been so different.

The principles instilled in me by my grandparents before being gang raped (I can say it now) I buried as anyone would who'd given up on life. I was lucky, an angel was provided just for me and I was able to survive. I no longer have the nightmares. I've forgiven them. All of them. In life we all do what we thinks best thing at the time.

And to the men and boys who raped me I pity you. I've forgiven you and pray no one close to you will ever experience what you did to me. I hope you can accept my forgiveness and heal yourselves.

To Mr. Wong. I forgive you. You did what you thought was in the best interest of the school and that time was different, 30 years ago, when as James Brown once said: *"It's a man's world."* I blamed you Mr. Wong for expelling me from high school. I'm so happy this book was not published sooner because it wouldn't show the understanding I have today.

I hope this book will bring to the fore, children are to be protected and institutions must not make decisions that jeopardise the children in order to save the reputation of some institution. A handful of boys could never have brought down the name of the school. The school had a great foundation and it would've recovered. It would've prevented this abuse from happening to anyone else.

To my English teacher, Mrs. Reid. In 2009 when I started writing this book I opened a door and faced all my past demons. Everyone said, I remembered everything from my past but the things I recall most vividly were the things I had locked safely away. When you took me to the Principal, you had no other choice, you had to do what you thought was right and in my best interest. You had no control over Mr. Wong's reactions. Still the day I opened the door, I was overcome and scared like a little child and to write this book, expressing my true feelings was in order to move forward. I apologize to you for how I felt. I wrote as the wounded child, today I apologise as the free woman I am.

Being nominated by The Jamaica Environment Trust and among five teachers for a champion teacher award, afforded us the perfect excuse to meet after speaking on Facebook for almost a year. It was with eager anticipation I invited you to attend the award ceremony and you agreed and as I rode the bus to Kingston alone I wrote the following:

"The last time I saw you was thirty five years ago when I walked out of Mr. Wong's office. I am sitting on the Knutsford Express on my way to Kingston where I will see you again face to face as you meet and transport me to the Award ceremony. We have been communicating this past year and have made peace with each other. The childhood picture I painted of you as this evil teacher who betrayed me has been erased and replaced as I see clearly that as a young teacher you did what you thought was in my best interest. Today you will stand beside me and support me in the

absence of my partner in life, who is unable to make the trip with me today. As the bus draws nearer I am extremely calm, I am a little worried and afraid, I promised Ian there would be no tears. I feel like I am finally meeting my mother. Did you know as a student in your class I admired you and often imagined you would adopt me? I smile as I finally release the memories of the last time I saw you .As those memories go I see love in your eyes and pain as you watched me leave the Principal's office. I did not see it then. I did not recognize it then, I do now.

We now have our future together. Finally the bus arrives and I see you standing there looking at the bus. My heart skips a beat. Please make her love me. I thought to myself. I step off the bus into your arms and you cried tears of joy. There was really no need for words. We both knew we found each other and it was ok. I won't let you go."

Unearthing the Diamond

Thank you for taking this trip with me...

Tamika Felina Pommells Williams

To my readers

Please do not feel sorry for me, I've been through a lot but I've had so many good things happen in my life. This book is a reality today because I decided to take action. Its now 2016 seven long years since I had written it. I tried every possible way to be published and nothing worked. I was referred to Chris by a friend who thought he'd help me with my business. I made contact and over several emails of sharing my frustrations of doing business in my country, suggested I publish an E-book. I casually mentioned I'd written my life story and was he interested in reading it. He said yes and then was disappointed since nothing materialized. I gave up and decided at least I'd written a book and felt it may never see the light of day.

One evening in April 2016 I wrote a post on Facebook stating: *"I had written a book and though I have tried several times to get it published, I have gotten no further than completing my manuscript. Anyone with ideas in helping me publishing my book, please inbox me."* There was a single response (publicly, not in a private message).

"This is what I do. My business is publishing budding authors." The message was from Author Kwame McPherson.

I have gone through so many emotions but one thing *is* constant. I am **NOT** afraid. Sometimes in life we just have to look at the answers to what we ask for and getting my story to the wider world was something I couldn't have done on my own. I told my husband earlier this year when the business picked up I'd self-publish my book, now it's the other way around. My rocky mountain paradise has become my sanctuary, wild birds pitch onto my hands and sit there as if I'm a tree; hummingbirds hover over me and it's totally unexplainable how we've taken a rocky hillside and made it into a garden where we share with the world.

Going through the trauma, some people may misunderstand you or why you hurt but if you open your eyes and see, there are people around eager to give love and support since none of us can do it alone. Fear has the ability to cripple us as if it were a train on tracks, running over and crushing our legs. I learnt to get over the fear of what people may think and so can you. People will always think negative things whether we know it or not.

And for me one of my fears in writing this book was about people knowing I was brutally gang raped and the shame I endured but there was another side to this story - I survived the many other challenges life threw at me, I was still able to touch the lives of others positively.

This brings us to choice. I could easily have chosen to remain a victim of life, instead with love, acceptance and guidance I've been able to rise up and create. The road hasn't been easy but when you're able to get up and breathe again - life is worth living. The little fifteen-year-old girl has grown up. I'm no longer a child, no longer a victim. I've been unearthed, chiseled and polished, shining brightly on my rocky mountain paradise.

Unearthing the Diamond

Everyday we awaken to new challenges and with love and acceptance of ourselves we make it to another day.

'The journey, will always be the journey; it's your perspective of your journey that matters'

Epilogue

'We made it!' was Ian's favourite quote. "We made it by the grace of God, hard work and the help of good friends."

We may have faltered and fell many times along the way but as the poem, Footprints: "My precious, precious child, it's in the difficult times that I carried you."

The web of life unfolds with every new day, touching so many lives as it branches off in all directions. Surround yourself with the right people with similar energies as yours. Protect this web at all cost. Life is a cycle. Out of every bad situation something good happens, look at my life as I come to the end of this book. We all have choices. I've chosen to take a positive from the negative and be complete, be whole.

I close by saying thanks to you, Ian, you taught me to be happy with myself, accept the teacher as well as the lesson. You planted me like a seed in the soil of life, nurturing me everyday, sometimes with gentle hands, sometimes with tough love. Now I'm in full bloom. *How do I say thanks for a lifetime of love?* Look at me and **be** Proud.

Tribute written to Ian December 14 2009 on your 56th birthday.

I knew you were the one for me, you mothered and fathered me but most of all you befriended me. You're so many things to me but most of all you're my best friend. You strengthen me when I'm weak and help me back on my feet. You say, "Don't quit, never settle for less." And sometimes I hated your voice of reason but in every situation you were proven to be right.

I am FREE!

You taught me the meaning of freedom. You said, "Do what you'll do but be true to yourself. Sleep with another if you like but never lie to me."

I don't wish to sleep with anyone but you. With the freedom you have given me I have enslaved myself to you.

Tamika Felina Pommells Williams

How could I wish to be free when you are my freedom? I'm free to release the child within! I'm free to speak. I'm free to share even silly things with you even when I know you'd rather meditate, or pray, but, you take time to listen to my silly thoughts. I've watched you change and grow in the 32 years we've been together and I used to think you were so strong because you seemed so unfeeling when you were younger but now I know it was because you had to protect me .It was a most difficult task being my man, husband, mother, father and friend.

Today, I recalled you buying me my first make up kit when I was eighteen-years-old. That was 30 years ago. You sat me down and applied the makeup, which I spoiled with my tears, because I thought I wasn't pretty enough for you. In your gentle way you explained I was now a woman and you wanted me to experience the little things women do. I didn't understand at the time but slowly over the years as I apply my makeup I realise it was the beginning of taking a little quiet time each day, just for me.

Unearthing the Diamond

I also look back and remember how you taught me about my body and how not to be ashamed of my curves and how to lovingly touch myself. How you did all that plus keeping your sanity and raising our son is still beyond me. Now, this morning, we awoke in our bed! Alone in our home and the happiness, peace and love I feel, cannot be measured.

Thank you Ian for loving me; for seeing me when I was blinded by my experiences, for caring and helping me to stay focused when I would've given up.

Thank you for teaching me to see the big picture - for separating the positives from the negatives.

I look forward to growing old with you. As you said a week ago, "I don't need to cheat on you Tamika because I never know which of you I'll awaken with each day." You continued by saying that I've changed my hairstyle so many times you've lost count.

I'm every woman!!

I'm indeed a work in progress and though I've had challenging experiences, I've triumphed over them all. My family is with me, I now have more support and now that I've let the negativity of my past go, I'm surrounded by so much love and support.

My TEACHER, Kwame McPherson, welcome!

I'm happy and content. I have my future ahead.

This is not....

THE END!

About The Author

Tamika Felina Pommells Williams

Tamika Felina Pommells Williams is a nature lover in every sense of the word, finding a natural alternative in controlling pests and seeing beauty not only in flowers but in ALL of nature. Her philosophy in life is: *"mending broken pieces"*, evident in the craft items made, some being beautiful and one of a kind crafts made from egg shells. She believes that if beauty is seen in something broken then it takes on new characteristics instead of flaws. She feels she was a broken piece that has been mended. With a teaching career spanning over 22 years began in 1988, where she officially left the classroom in 2009 but now her garden *is* her classroom. Tamika has been nominated by the Jamaica Environmental programme; Champion Teacher Chairman of the Board Gutters Basic School; Owner and operator of the award-winning Ahhh...Ras Natango Gallery and Garden eco-Tourism Entity in Montego Bay; member of Jamaica Hotel and Tourist Association, member of The American Chamber of Commerce listed as number one in four categories on Trip Advisor Cottage Industry. The business has also taught employees to create Jamaican crafts for sale to visitors. The business, as member of the St James Horticultural Society is a regular winner of the medium garden category along with numerous awards for different classes in the floral exhibition. In addition, Tamika initiated the adoption of the local elementary school, Buckingham Primary School and supplies the school with art and other goods. She is actively involved in community building and sponsors the local Police Station in Granville St James. Tamika is affectionately called Mammy by the many people who visit her for assistance in one way or another. She credits her greatest achievements as being Mother and wife, being an amateur photographer and is passionate about taking pictures of nature. Her hobbies are gardening, cooking singing, taking photos and dancing and lately has added **author to her long list of accomplishments**!

To contact Tamika:
Telephone: (+1 876) 578 2582/807 4347

Unearthing the Diamond

Email: Tamika@rasnatango.com, tamikafelina@gmail.com

www.ingramcontent.com/pod-product-compliance
Lightning Source LLC
Chambersburg PA
CBHW021226090426
42740CB00006B/407